Jean Randier

MARINE NAVIGATION INSTRUMENTS

Translated from the French by John E. Powell

JOHN MURRAY

It is better to have absolutely no idea where one is, and to know it,
than to believe confidently that one is where one is not. CASSINI

Armillary sphere from Cosmographia
by Gemma Frisius. The Earth is at the
centre. The position of the equinoctial
colure, in other words the position of the
vernal equinox on the ecliptic, indicates
when the sphere was made. The
equinoctial and solstitial colures are of
course at right angles to one another.
These spheres – which derived their name
from the armilla, or bracelet – were
simple and clear at first and gave rough
and ready solutions to some of the
problems of navigation and astronomy,
but over the centuries they became
increasingly complicated and ornate
until eventually they were of no use at
all.

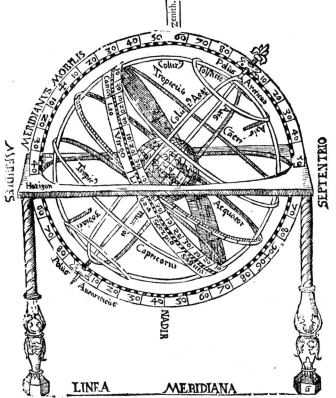

First published in Great Britain 1980
by John Murray, 50 Albemarle Street, London

Phototypeset by Keyspools Ltd, Golborne, Lancashire.
Printed in Italy

© Creative Publishing Marine 1977
English translation © John Murray (Publishers) Ltd 1980

ISBN 0 7195 3733 9

Contents

Introduction 5

1 Dead Reckoning 7
Out of Sight of Land, 7. Bound Lodestones, 10. The Steering Compass, 15. The Bearing Compass, 23. The Compensated Compass, 28. The Perfecting of the Magnetic Compass, 37. Dromoscopes and Dromographs, 38. Measuring the Distance Sailed, 40. From the Log Ship to the Patent Log, 40. Determining the Ship's Position, 56. The Chart and Plotting the Course, 56. Mariners' Quadrants, 62. Nautical Works, 65.

2 Practical Pilotage 68
The Pilot's Art, 68. Taking Soundings, 69. To See Afar in Order to Foresee, 73.

3 Celestial Navigation 76
Spheres, 77. The Cosmolabe, 78. Taking the Altitude, 82. Early Instruments for Measuring Angles, 82. The Mariner's Astrolabe, 83. The Gunter Quadrant, 86. The Cross-staff, 87. The Back-staff, 89. Reflecting Instruments, 93. Finding the Position by Astronomic Means, 105. Observations Without a Horizon, 114. The Art of Navigating by the Moon, 123. The Reflecting Circle, 125.

4 Time at Sea 134
Sand-glasses, 138. Sundials, 142. The Azimuth Dial, 143. The Analemmatic Dial, 144. The Diptych Dial, 145. The Equinoctial Dial, 146. The Horizontal Plate Dial, 146. The Vertical Dial, 148. The Polar Dial, 148. Sundials to Show Mean Time, 156. The Ring Dial, 157. The Equinoctial Ring Dial, 160. The Nocturnal, 166. Marine Chronometers, 173.

5 Hydrography, Geodesy and Terrestrial Astronomy 190
Angle Measurements, 191. Accurate Plotting, 194. Magnetic Inclination, 196. The Theodolite, 198. Measuring Circles, 199. Marine Astronomy on Land, 202.

6 Observing and Forecasting the Weather 204
Meteorological Instruments, 204. Barometric Pressure, 207. The Speed and Direction of the Wind, 211.

Alphabetical Index of the Instruments Illustrated 214
Bibliography 216
Acknowledgements 218
Sources of the Photographs 218
Museums and Collections 219

Introduction

The design and use of navigational instruments of the past always provide the seaman and the naval historian with food for thought, because the crude results obtained reflect methods of calculation that, though often forgotten, mark important and ingenious stages in the thinking behind the mariner's art.

This work is therefore an illustrated history of maritime navigation viewed through the pilot's 'tools'. It opens with the first recorded rational attempts by navigators to shape a course and determine their position at sea. It closes with the arrival of electricity, radio and electronics on the bridge at the beginning of this century. This was the point at which navigational instruments ceased to be specifically nautical and assimilated well-tried aerial and terrestrial techniques.

Naval historians apart, there are today a great many collectors of navigational instruments. It was with them in mind that we produced this book in the form of an iconography that will help the reader identify pieces he may come across.

The work is divided according to theme into six chapters covering the various aspects of the subject – coastal and deep-sea pilotage, the measurement of time, hydrography, astronomy and meteorology.

However complete and logical this list is intended to be, it cannot encompass the vast and highly varied range of nautical scientific instruments produced by engineers and artists, designers and instrument makers.

The bibliography should enable the reader to draw more deeply from the fund of information that is increasing daily with the discovery of further pieces spotted at auctions, in private collections or in museums.

The nautical heritage is vast, but with the relentless passage of time it has been scattered to the four winds. With the present revival of interest and enthusiasm for the history of the sea, however, there is every chance that the efforts now again being made in the field of naval archaeology will meet with success. This book is but one element in that immense undertaking.

Any remarks or suggestions on the best way of conserving this 'imaginary maritime museum' would be most welcome.

Jean Randier

1. Portuguese sea compass, mounted in gimbals, 1764. Paper compass card, bowl decorated by hand. There are two openings and a style mounted on the cap for taking bearings.

1 · Dead Reckoning

HYDROGRAPHIE
DV P. G. FOVRNIER.
LIVRE ONZIESME.

De la Bouſſole, & des vertus admirables de l'Aymant.

Que l'vſage en eſt tres ancien.

CHAP. PREMIER.

PAR ce mot de Bouſſole, que nous appellons d'ordinaire Quadran, & sur la Mediterranée Calamite, i'entends vn Inſtrument duquel les Mariniers ſe ſeruent pour ſe conduire ſur Mer, par le moyen d'vn fer aymanté qui eſt dedans, & qui ſe tournant touſiours vers le Nord, leur monſtre quelle route ils tiennent.

Nos anciens François la nommoient Marinette, comme nous voyons dans les Antiquitez de Fauchet, lequel au liure de l'Origine de la Langue & Poeſie Françoiſe, rapporte les vers que Guyot de Prouines compoſa enuiron l'an 1200. ou peu deuant, auſquels apres auoir parlé du Pole Arctique, il dit

2. Hydrographie, by Father Fournier, 1643. Head-piece to the eleventh volume.

Out of Sight of Land

The history of navigation before the 15th century rests largely on conjecture. Occasional remarks in descriptions of the voyages of St. Paul or Marco Polo allow us a glimpse of a sounding lead here or a primitive compass there without, however, revealing whether there was any real method behind their use.

The accounts of Mediterranean voyages during the Middle Ages tell of adventurous seamen setting out for the Levant without chart, compass or instrument for measuring altitudes (an astrolabe). All they had to rely on was some idea of the successive headlands to be rounded between short stretches offshore and a lead for measuring the depth of water to avoid running aground.

But with navigation, as with any other technique, discoveries are made and new methods developed only when progress becomes an absolute necessity. After the short stages of Mediterranean passages, where the reassuring presence of land was never far below the horizon, voyages in the Atlantic were a totally new adventure, with their abstract courses across blank charts.

3. *Dry-card compass, Leghorn, Italy, 1719. Note the old system of notation: P for 'ponente' (West) and a cross to the East as a reminder of the direction of Jerusalem. The card is graduated in degrees by quadrants. Bowl and cover in wood.*

The Chinese astrological compass, called a lo-pan, was also used for divining the future and is thus complicated by additional concentric circles of esoteric symbols. Nevertheless, in the centre will be found the rudimentary nautical rose of 24 rhumbs (tchéou), the main points being indicated by three bands of one, two or three vertical identification marks. The meaning of the symbols on the compass remain rather obscure, the ideograms representing philosophical and religious concepts of the Far East.

As in the early days of European navigation, the helmsman must keep the cardinal direction (south for the Chinese) opposite the rhumb corresponding to the heading chosen. This rhumb therefore itself constitutes the lubber's line. The habit of using such roses divided into 24 parts (or 12 in the case of Japanese compasses) was so deeply rooted that it is not unusual to find 19th-century Asian compass roses mounted in the European fashion – a compass card with a pivot and cap – but graduated in both 360° and 24 rhumbs. In fact this was common practice for a long time in Europe as well, the card being divided into 32 rhumbs of the wind. ►

The principles of the charts and instruments of the Venetians must have reached the early Portuguese seamen who explored the coast of Africa. The discovery of the Canary Islands by Lanzarote Malocello dates back to 1386. Once the position of the islands had been 'fixed', instruments for determining latitude and direction had to be used to return to them.

The first serious studies of navigation date from the time of Henry the Navigator (1394–1460), one of the sons of King John I of Portugal and founder of the school of Sagres at the beginning of the 15th century. This was the school that trained many great pilots and, by its teaching, probably made possible the voyage of Vasco da Gama to Mozambique and India in 1497.

At one time it was intellectually convenient to describe the voyage of da Gama as hazardous coasting. In the *Histoire générale de la navigation*, however, Marguet mentions a 'roteiro', or pilot book, published in Oporto in 1838 which attempts to retrace the route followed by the great Portuguese mariner. It claims that by following the coast as far as Mina (on the Ivory Coast) via the Cape Verde Islands, a ship would take 78 days to reach St. Helena Bay near the Cape of Good Hope. However, such a rapid passage would be quite impossible to achieve by following the coast as claimed, which proves that an offshore route must have been chosen like that followed by d'Entrecasteaux in 1791–1792 and Baudin in 1800, who took 74 and 77 days respectively. On these voyages the Equator had to be crossed at 20° West to keep clear of the north-setting current and the tropical calms.

Navigation by dead reckoning had thus become a reality. It presupposed a certain number of tools, a methodology and what we nowadays tend to call 'options' concerning the shape of the Earth. The idea of the flat map, planisphere or *mappa mundi* – the representation of the Earth on a flat surface – has exercised the minds of geographers and travellers for centuries. But more of that later. Suffice it to say that the idea of navigating by polar co-ordinates – angle and distance run – made sense on a plane map of the

8

continued on page 12

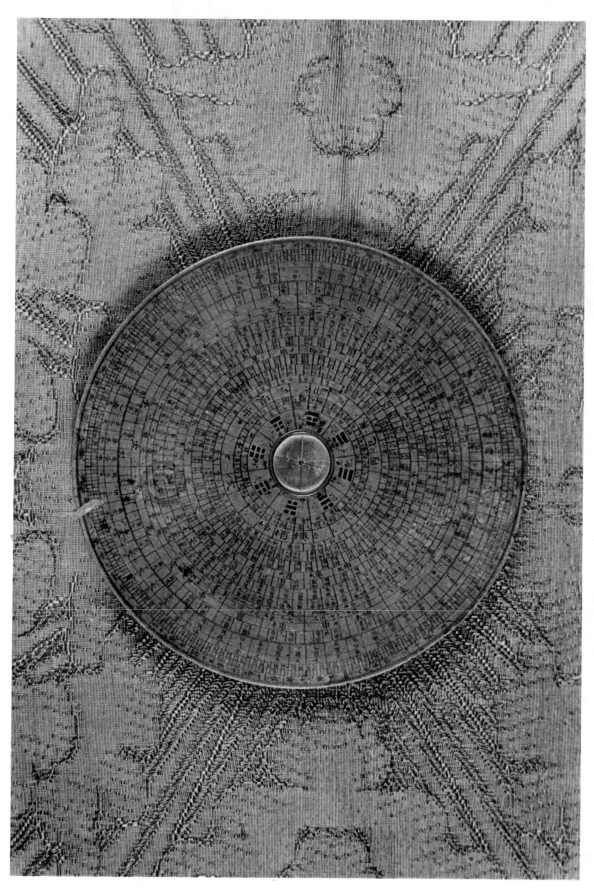

Bound Lodestones

According to the history books lodestones first appeared in China, but navigation does not seem to have been the first use for this oxide of iron (magnetite, Fe_3O_4). Because of its magical properties the stone seemed to be destined mainly for use in occult and esoteric sciences and its nautical application came relatively late. Marco Polo mentioned it around 1280, but so too did the Scandinavian Sagas of the same period. Be that as it may, until magnetic fields could be induced artificially by means of coils and electrical currents the lodestone was the only means of 'refreshing' steel compass needles and it is understandable that the stones should have been set in very ornate or even precious mountings to form what we call today 'bound lodestones'.

There was much mistrust of the peculiar effects of these stones. In 1586 Polter wrote that different 'magnets' magnetised iron in different ways, which was the reason why navigators took several with them so that they could obtain the best average magnetisation of the compass. Bound lodestones were also in widespread use on land. From the 18th century onwards high quality steel bars that could be given lasting magnetisation, and hence were called permanent magnets, were in use alongside lodestones.

The Steering Compass

The theory that the primitive Asian compass was passed on to the Arabs by the Chinese during their seasonal voyages to India and the Persian Gulf and then 'imported' into Europe by the Venetians via the merchants of the Levant is now contested by historians; in their opinion the compass is of Scandinavian origin and was introduced into the Mediterranean by the Norsemen in the 11th century.

The old French name for a lodestone, *calamite*, comes from *calamus*, the Latin word for a straw, which, if tradition is to be believed, was filled with powdered iron oxide and then floated in a bowl of water.

Magnet and *magnetite* are said to be derived from Magnesia, the name of a region of Ionia where the mineral was plentiful. However, the French word *aimant* (*iman* in Spanish) is explained by the attraction, literally 'amorous', of the stone to iron. In *Instrumentos nauticos en el Museo Naval*, Salvator Garcia Franco records the Indian, Chinese and Japanese names with the same meaning of a 'stone attracted to iron'. The Arabs, for their part, called the magnet a 'guide', and those who lead the believers, after the manner of the Prophet, bear the name of the magic stone. This is also the sense adopted in English – *lodestone* or *leadstone*, the stone that guides. The more pragmatic Dutch call it simply *zeilsteen*, literally 'sailing stone'.

From the straw filled with iron oxide to the magnetised steel needle seems no more than a step; tradition has it that the breakthrough was made at

9. Boat's compass, around 1860, signed 'Vinay à Paris', No. 2604. Mica compass card 138 mm in diameter, marked 'Marine impériale'. Within the mahogany binnacle is a curved brass plate painted white to reflect the light from the paraffin lamp, which is mounted on a track to illuminate the card. Instead of the traditional pivot and cap, this compass has a vertical spindle attached to the compass card, the lower pivot turning in a jewelled bearing and the upper pivot being guided by a cross bar (visible in the photograph). The spindle may be raised by means of a locking device in order to prevent wear.

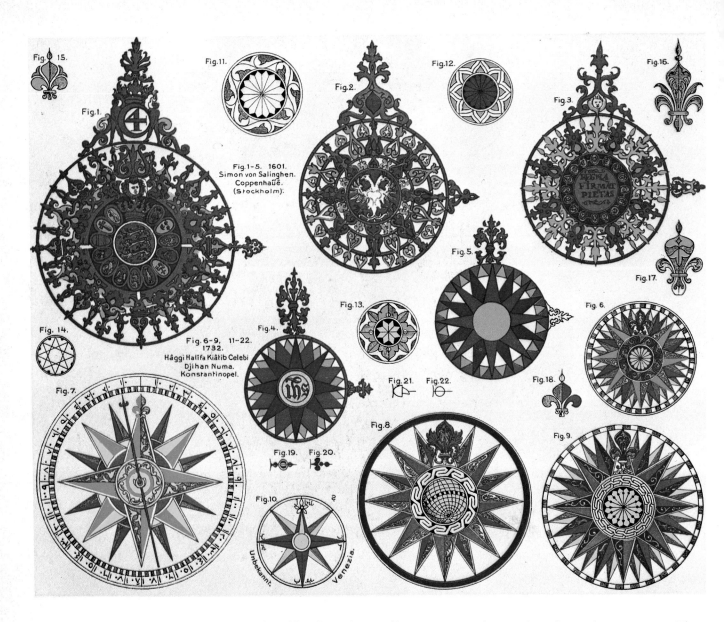

Fig. 15.

Fig. 11.

Fig. 1.

Fig. 2.

Fig. 12.

Fig. 16.

Fig. 3.

Fig. 1–5. 1601.
Simon von Salinghen.
Coppenhaue.
(Stockholm).

Fig. 17.

Fig. 5.

Fig. 14.

Fig. 6–9, 11–22.
1732.
Hâggi Halîfa Kiâtib Celebi
Djihan Numa.
Konstantinopel.

Fig. 13.

Fig. 6.

Fig. 4.

Fig. 7.

Fig. 21.   Fig. 22.

Fig. 18.

Fig. 19.   Fig. 20.

Fig. 8.

Fig. 9.

Fig. 10.

Unbekannt.

Venezia.

Compass cards. Plate reproduced from
Der Kompass *by Capt. Schück.*

Amalfi, where the needle was mounted on a pivot for easier use at sea. Then in the 15th century came the mounting of the card on the needle, which truly 'marinised' the instrument.

Initially the compass was placed in a round bowl of turned wood, but at the end of the 16th century it is to be found mounted in an assembly of three square, gimballed boxes. The middle box was to disappear, leaving only the gimbal ring, and later still, with the introduction of beaten copper, would come round, lead-weighted bowls for dry compasses and, *a fortiori*, liquid compasses. Around 1700 it was noted in the proceedings of the French Academy of Science that the effects of variation were not the same in wooden boxes as in brass ones, which were suspected of containing iron impurities. La Hire suggested bowls of marble! But the copper bowl had its supporters. The astronomer Arago had observed that the oscillations of the needle died down more quickly over a copper plate; this was therefore taken into account.

The continued use of square boxes, in spite of being illogical with round cards, is explained by the fact that they fitted very conveniently into the square recesses of the steering compass binnacle, the lubber's line thereby aligning itself automatically.

16

10. *Dry-card overhead or tell-tale compass of the French Restoration period. The gimballed suspension is carved in the form of a rope. The bowl is decorated with anchors and dolphins.*

The design of the compass needle long preoccupied compass-makers and theoreticians in magnetism alike. The phenomenon of magnetic variation, which was slight in Europe in the 15th century, was at first believed to be due to either a defect in the metal or the form of the needle itself. Over the centuries this led to a profusion of strange shapes – oval, lozenge-shaped, forked (which it was claimed would eliminate variation altogether) and V-shaped (Crescentius, 1607). But eventually variation had to be accepted for what it was, an error varying from one place to another and considerable in some, as was to be proved by the great voyages.

The concept of lines of equal variation, in principle easy enough to determine by measuring the two directions compass North and true North (from the pole star), led to the idea of fixing the ship's position by measuring the variation and locating the corresponding isogonic line on the globe. This geometric line and the latitude together were supposed to give an accurate position. In France the best known treatise on this method is *la Mécométrie de l'aymant* by Guillaume le Nautonnier of Castlefranc-sur-Lot, 1603. Unfortunately many preconceived ideas about the 'natural geometry of the world' led to lines of equal variation being confused with terrestrial meridians and wrongly plotted. In addition nothing precise was known

12. 17th- and 18th-century compass cards and needles. Reproduced from Der Kompass *by Capt. A. Schück.* ►

about the dip of the needle, first mentioned by Robert Norman in 1580, and even less about the change in variation at any one place over time.

The permanent magnetisation of compass needles posed a serious problem because the steel used was relatively soft. Moreover, the ability of the needle to overcome drag caused by the motion of the ship is proportional to the magnetic couple of the needle, and hence to its mass. Where weight is involved there is also the problem of increased friction between the cap and the pivot. It was not long before pivots were being made of steel, which gave way to iridium in the nineteenth century, while caps were fitted with jewelled bearings of agates and rubies.

Compass makers continued to be concerned about the shape of needles and the 19th century saw the development of Duchemin's ring magnet, which was strongly magnetised and had greater residual magnetism. Coulomb proved that the hole for the cap and the shape of the needle were

11. Three dry-card compasses. Top left: regulation design, marked 'Marine impériale', printed in black on corozo. Centre: large compass card on corozo. Right: light card of the Thomson kind consisting of tissue paper, an aluminium ring and four bar magnets, the whole assembly suspended by silk threads. Made by D. Doignon, early 20th century.

not important; all that mattered was the weight of steel. But what a debate there had been before that! Van Zwinden, a Frisian professor, favoured a straight, slightly flattened steel wire. Fleurieu recommended a straight flattened bar, 7 or 8 mm wide and 16 cm long. In 1772 Borda proposed a set of four steel bar magnets. This system had, in fact, been developed by the Dane Lous, who mounted four needles on a wooden board, each 153 mm by 4 mm and 2.5 mm in section, and spaced over 62 mm overall. The device weighed 48 grams and, when deflected through 90°, took 7.5 seconds to come to rest. Coulomb adopted the system, suggested that the weight be

18

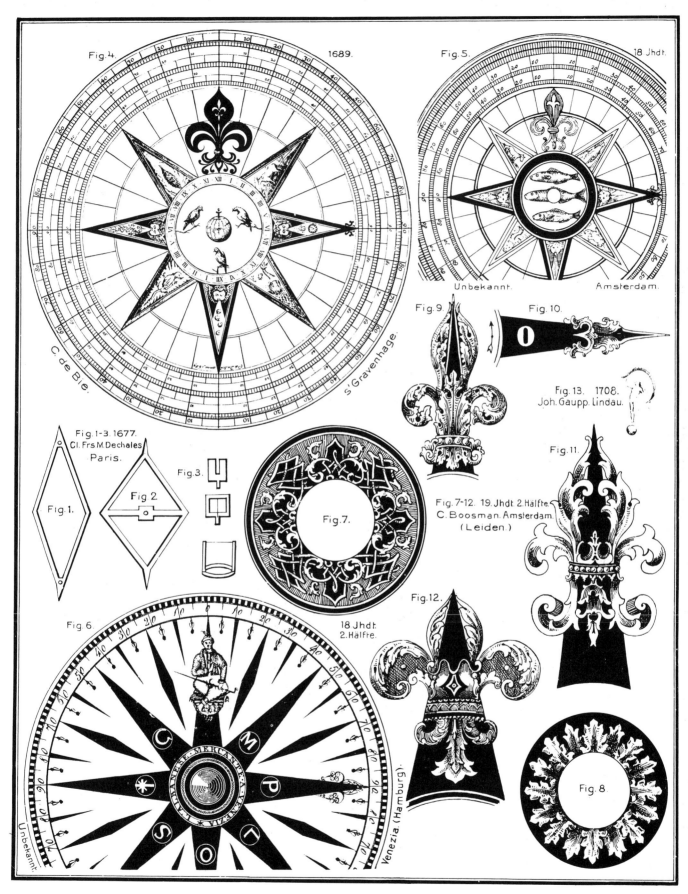

Fig. 4.   1689.   Fig. 5.   18 Jhdt.

C. de Bie.   s'Gravenhage.   Unbekannt.   Amsterdam.

Fig. 9.   Fig. 10.

Fig. 1-3. 1677.
Cl. Frs M. Dechales.
Paris.   Fig. 3.

Fig. 2   Fig. 13.   1708.
Fig. 1.   Joh. Gaupp. Lindau.

Fig. 11.

Fig. 7.   Fig. 7-12. 19. Jhdt. 2. Hälfte.
C. Boosman. Amsterdam.
(Leiden.)

Fig. 12.

Fig. 6.   18 Jhdt.
2. Hälfte.

Fig. 8.

Unbekannt.   Venezia. (Hamburg).

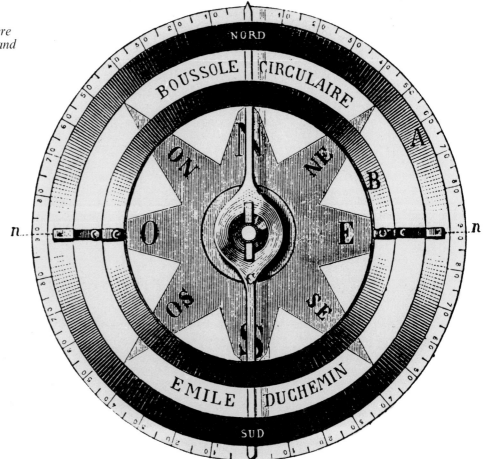

13. Ring magnet compass by E. Duchemin. Compasses of this type were tested on naval vessels between 1873 and 1875 and a number were ordered.

14. Plate reproduction from Der Kompass *by Capt. Schück showing various types of compass cards and some needle systems in common use in the 18th and 19th centuries.* ▶

reduced to 32 grams and produced a construction diagram. However, it was the Thomson dry-card compass of 1876 that finally put an end to the arguments. The shape of the magnets was no longer an issue – without exception they were now cylindrical bars of drawn steel wire, 6 or 8 in number arranged in pairs suspended by a system of silk threads and attached to a very light paper card, the whole assembly weighing less than 20 grams.

The liquid compass, which was being produced commercially by about 1880, put an end to the problem of friction. It was the work of Dent (1833) and Ritchie (1855), which led to the construction of the first liquid compasses. Henceforth the card was fixed to a circular float in a bowl filled with a non-freezing liquid such as alcohol or glycerine (something of a throw-back to the earliest sea compass). As the assembly was in perfect equilibrium in accordance with Archimedes' principle, the cap now only had to guide the card around the pivot. Furthermore, these compasses were fitted with a strong bar magnet, so that they were unaffected by drag due to the motion of the ship; they were excellent in small ships that were lively in heavy weather and later proved ideal in powered vessels prone to vibration.

The gyroscopic compass, which came into general service in fighting fleets just after the first world war and in the merchant navy after the second, made the magnetic compass seem rather antiquated, although it was made obligatory to carry a standard compass of the traditional type; it is, in fact, still used aboard both warships and merchant vessels.

Let us now return to the early compass cards. The numerous examples reproduced here, particularly those drawn from the book by Capt. Schück, give a good idea of the wide variety of designs from different countries and,

20

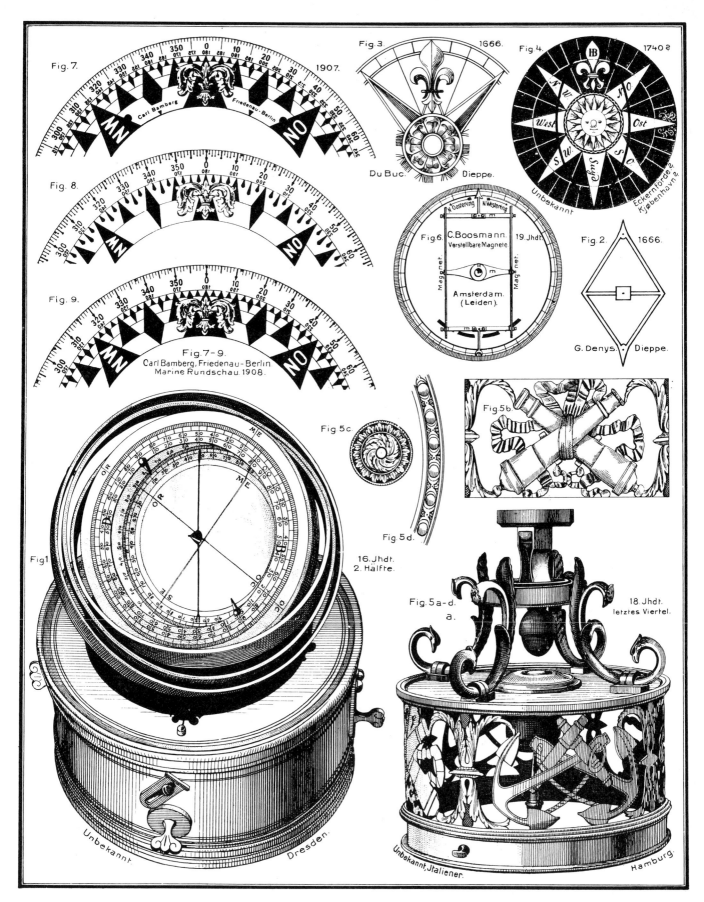

Fig. 7. 1907. Carl Bamberg Friedenau-Berlin

Fig. 8.

Fig. 9.
Fig. 7–9.
Carl Bamberg, Friedenau-Berlin
Marine Rundschau. 1908.

Fig. 3. 1666.
Du Buc. Dieppe.

Fig. 4. 1740 ?
N O
N W N O
West Ost
S W S O
S ud
Unbekannt
Eckernförde 2.
Kjøbenhavn 2.

Fig. 6. C. Boosmann. 19. Jhdt.
Verstellbare Magnete
N Oostering N Westering
Magnet. Magnet.
m m
Amsterdam.
(Leiden).

Fig. 2. 1666.
G. Denys. Dieppe.

Fig. 5 c.

Fig. 5 b.

Fig. 5 d.
16. Jhdt.
2. Hälfte.

Fig 1

Unbekannt. Dresden.

Fig. 5 a–d.
a.

Unbekannt, Jtaliener.

18. Jhdt.
letztes Viertel.

Hamburg.

21

15. *English compass card by Dollond, London, 18th century.*

in some cases, different periods within the same country. However, the general arrangement of European compass roses rests upon a number of fundamental invariables. The Arab sidereal rose of 32 points prevailed over the Chinese cosmogonic rose of 12 or 24 points, although the rose in the great 'Roteiro' of 1483 by Garcie Ferrande had 24 divisions. In western Europe the 32 rhumbs of the wind first gained favour. The English word *compass* derives from the drawing instrument of the same name used for drawing these 'compass roses'. While on the subject of etymology, the origin of the French word for compass – *boussole* – remains obscure. The Spaniards, who call it *brújula*, think that the name comes from *bruja* (sorceress), but *buxha* (box), from the Greek, is another possibility.

The 32 divisions of $11\frac{1}{4}°$ each, or rhumbs (*rumbos* in Spanish), bear the names of the four cardinal points – Tramontana (N.), Ostro (S.), Levante (E.) and Ponente (W.) – the directions from which the principal winds of the Mediterranean blew – Libeccio (from Libya), Sirocco (from Syria), Greco (from Greece) – and a number of names invented for reasons of symmetry. Since 1932, by international agreement, compass cards have shown only the conventional initials N, S, E, W, plus occasionally the intermediate points NE, SW, etc.; as early as 1900, however, points notation was giving way to graduation in degrees.

Paper compass cards printed from a copper plate and sometimes embellished in colour began to appear with the development of engraving in the middle of the sixteenth century. These were glued initially onto card, but later onto mica or talc (silicate of magnesium), which held their shape and were unaffected by humidity or heat. From the end of the 19th century onwards cards were printed on corozo (or vegetable ivory), a transparent material suitable for liquid compasses and for illumination from below, the base of the bowl being fitted with glass.

The blobs of sealing wax or lead weights that are found on some old cards served to counteract the vertical component of the Earth's magnetic field.

The Bearing Compass

Also called the variation compass, the bearing compass was first used to measure the variation of the compass by comparing the position of the sun at midday, or that of the pole star, with the North-South line of the compass.

A thread stretched over the outer square box holding the compass was all that was needed for such a comparison between the North-South line and the shadow of the sun at midday. Nevertheless, from the 16th century onwards the triple-box, gimballed compass was fitted with six aligned windows, complete with sighting wires, through which bearings of objects on shore could be taken. It was quickly noticed that three-point bearings, however accurately observed, gave a large 'cocked hat' for want of precise knowledge about deviation and variation, particularly as the compass was often moved about the deck to places where observations were easier. It would be placed on something soft (a coil of rope or a bundled sail) and the bearing would be taken by two observers, one sighting the object and the other noting the reading.

The 'azimuth' compass with the alidade pivoting on the rim through an arc of 90° underwent some improvement, but it remained a very primitive, portable instrument. Pezenas describes it in *Astronomie des marins* in 1766 and it is still holding its own in the *Cours de navigation* by Bézout in 1814.

Incredible as it may seem, however, the triple-box, gimballed compass with sights is still being described in 1835 in the *Vade-mecum du marin* by Guépratte and it is not until 1870 that we find, in the *Cours de navigation* by Caillet and Dubois, a description of a permanently positioned variation compass with a pin-hole alidade attached to a pivot at the centre of the verge glass. The English 'standard compass' had left its mark.

Compasses with centrally pivoted, pin-hole alidades had existed, however, since the end of the 18th century, as the surviving examples prove. After all, was it not logical to apply the alidade of the astrolabe to a horizontal scale? Perhaps the main problem was cutting holes in the centre of the glass.

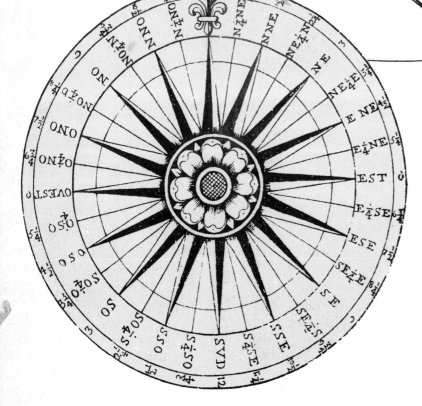

16. *Dry compass card graduated into points; from* Science et pratique du pilotage *by Yves Valois.*

17. Above: *18th-century azimuth or bearing compass. Reproduced from* Pratique du pilotage *by Father Pezenas. Alidades of this type, turning on the rim over an arc of 90°, were manufactured until the middle of the 19th century even though the central alidade was already in existence in the 17th century. However, like many other tools of navigation, this archaic instrument became hallowed by tradition or, rather, by the daily routine of seamen accustomed to doing things a certain way. In the model shown the horizontal arm was placed diametrically, in other words across the centre of the card, and the entire instrument was then turned until a landmark bore or the shadow cast by the thread aligned correctly. The angle read from the compass card was then the azimuth. Alternatively, if the box was aligned with the fore-and-aft line of the ship, a bearing between 0 and 90° could be taken in relation to the compass course, which was indicated by the lubber's line.*

Compass cards. Plate reproduced from Der Kompass *by Capt. Schück.*

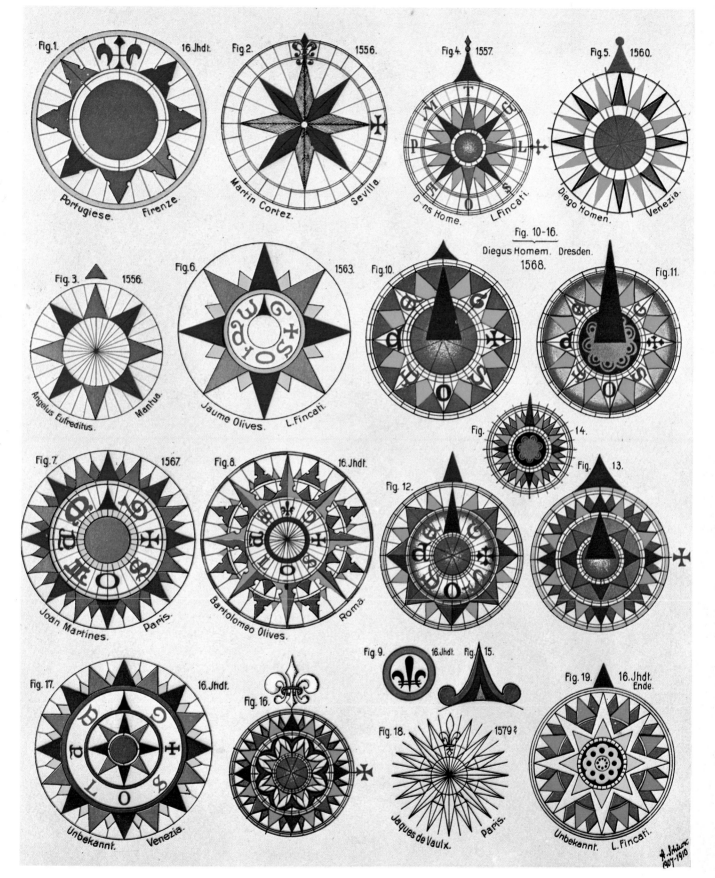

Fig.1. 16.Jhdt. Portugiese. Firenze.

Fig 2. 1556. Martin Cortez. Sevilla.

Fig.4. 1557. D..ns Home. L.Fincati.

Fig.5. 1560. Diego Homen. Venezia.

Fig.3. 1556. Angelus Eufreditus. Mantua.

Fig.6. 1563. Jaume Olives. L.Fincati.

Fig. 10-16.
Diegus Homem. Dresden.
1568.

Fig.10. Fig.11.

Fig. 14.

Fig. 12. Fig. 13.

Fig.7. 1567. Joan Martines. Paris.

Fig.8. 16.Jhdt. Bartolomeo Olives. Roma.

Fig. 17. 16.Jhdt. Unbekannt. Venezia.

Fig. 16.

Fig. 9. 16.Jhdt. Fig. 15.

Fig. 18. 1579? Jaques de Vaulx. Paris.

Fig. 19. 16.Jhdt. Ende. Unbekannt. L.Fincati.

A.Schück
1907-1910

25

18. *Multi-purpose dry-card compass from the reign of Louis XVI, as the carrying handles show. The card is printed from a copper plate (Bertin sculpt.) and is marked 'Le Graveran-La Rochelle', although it is not clear whether this is the maker of the card or of the whole instrument. Two apertures set in the axis of the case allow bearings of landmarks to be taken. A shade is provided for use when the horizon is very bright. A pivoted mirror attached above the card is used for measuring the azimuths of heavenly bodies. The shades are for viewing the sun direct.*

19. *Bearing compass of the dry-card type made by Chardon in 1779. The coloured paper card is printed from a copper plate. When taking observations the instrument is raised above its walnut case by means of the two side supports holding the gimbals, which are locked when not in use. The compass box has two sighting apertures with sight-wires. A red shade is provided. The rose bears an inscription in French reading 'New reflecting variation compass. Approved by the Royal Academy of Science. By Monsieur De Gaulle of the Royal Academy of Science of Rouen and hydrographer in Le Havre, from whom this instrument may be obtained. None is sold without having been tested at sea. 1779'.*

20. *Variation compass, unsigned, 1726. Card drawn by hand. There are two tensioners for the sight wires and a red shade for taking direct sights. Dimensions: 325 × 325 × 255 mm.*

21. *When the instrument (No. 19) is lowered to the bottom of the case on its sliding supports the very ingenious device shown here, which consists of four ivory rods supporting a brass plate under the card itself, takes the weight of the card and thus prevents wear of the point of the pivot. The lead ring, which appears to be oxidised, is the counterweight of the compass bowl.*

The Compensated Compass

The phenomenon of compass deviation aboard ships – errors caused by the proximity of iron – was recognised from 1650 onwards but deliberately ignored as no way had been found of taking it into account. In 1801 Matthew Flinders tackled the problem on the *Investigator* and suggested a cure using a bar of soft iron. This device, which is called simply the 'Flinders bar', is still part of the equipment of Thomson-type binnacles. The cupboard-type binnacle continued to house the steering compasses, and it was this fixture that served as a basis for Barlow's research in 1824 that culminated in the first system of compensating spheres, and for the more general and theoretical studies on the effects of hard and soft iron in ships carried out by the mathematician Denis Poisson (1781–1840). Finally, the practical research on compensation by the English mathematician Archibald Smith led to the well-known formula which is still universally employed. The names of other marine scientists, such as Johnson, Airy and Scoresby, are also associated with work concerning magnetism; their efforts obviously assumed immense importance, as the uncompensated magnetic compass was so erratic aboard iron ships that it was totally useless.

It was the work of Sir William Thomson (Lord Kelvin) that led to the invention of the familiar binnacle for steering and bearing compasses. A tall wooden column supports the compass at a convenient height for sighting through the alidade. It is protected by a hood and has brackets on the

Lord Kelvin (Sir William Thomson).

Small magnetic compass binnacle for a coaster or yacht. English, end of the 19th century. Iron spheres attached to the brackets, corrector magnets housed in the column in radial recesses at right angles to one another under the beading fixed in accordance with the generators of the column.

Large Thomson-type compensating binnacle with spheres on the outside and permanent transverse and longitudinal magnets housed in the column. On the front of the binnacle can be seen the corrector called the Flinders bar. The column also contains electrical illumination and a system for correcting heeling errors. The brass hood includes a paraffin lamp for emergency lighting. Note that the lugs of the base-plate have elongated holes so that the lubber's line can be adjusted precisely by pivoting the entire column through a few degrees.

outside for the compensating spheres and the Flinders bar. Inside the column are the transverse and longitudinal permanent magnets and, in the centre, the heeling error magnet that was indispensable on sailing ships, which remained on the same tack for many weeks in the trade winds.

22. *Boat's compass, inscribed on the verge ring 'Boussole à relèvements, perfectionnée par P. Touboulic – Brest n° 20'. This is a Second Empire (c.1860) regulation compass with a Duchemin ring magnet. A mirror is attached to the centrally pivoted alidade so that the graduations can be read while sighting the object.*

23. *'Land on the port bow!' A scene from life aboard a French sail training ship, about 1880. It was common at that time to set up a tripod-mounted bearing compass on a clear part of the poop deck to take bearings of landmarks, in total disregard of all the considerations about deviation caused by the ship's iron, such as artillery, metallic mast fittings, etc. Etching by Léon Paris.*

24. *Binnacle for two compasses with a central compartment for a lantern. This was a convenient arrangement for the helmsman, as he always had a reference compass before his eyes whichever side of the helm he stood, but it had the serious disadvantage that each compass affected the other. In 1730 Duhamel du Monceau and Bigot de Morogue drew attention to the effect of the compasses on each other and in 1760 d'Après de Mannevilette estimated it at between 5° and 6° on the basis of precise calculations. A decade later the hydrographer De Gaulle discovered reciprocal deviation of up to 26° on some vessels. We know, however, that variation was still very controversial at that time. Pedro de Medina had even flatly denied its existence in his* Arte de navegar *of 1545.*

25. *Dry-card compass with brass binnacle and compensators for mounting on a stand aboard small merchant vessels or pleasure craft, by G. Heckelmann, Hamburg.*

Wooden binnacle for a sailing ship in the coastal trade, with three compartments to house two compasses and a lantern. In front of the binnacle are three dry-card compasses of the 18th and 19th centuries.

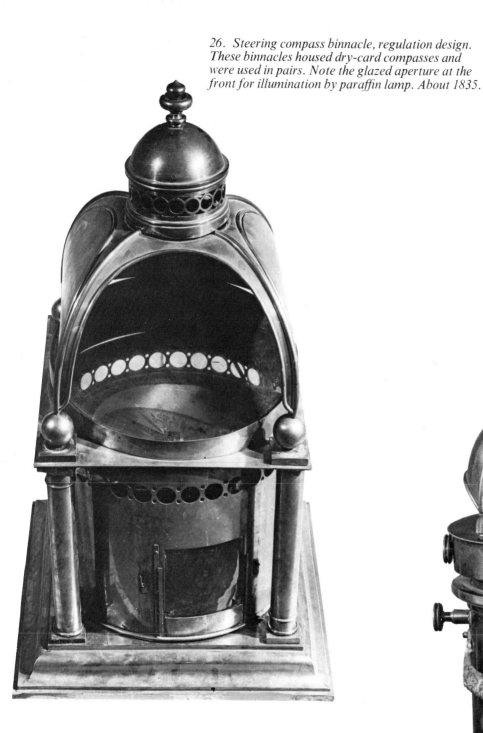

26. Steering compass binnacle, regulation design. These binnacles housed dry-card compasses and were used in pairs. Note the glazed aperture at the front for illumination by paraffin lamp. About 1835.

27. Steering compass by Pellegrin, regulation equipment in the French Navy during the Empire and the Restoration (early 19th century). Note the thirty second sand-glass hung under the hood.

28. *Boat's compass by E. Dent & Co.,
51, Strand & 4, Royal Exchange,
London. Width of the binnacle 22 cm,
total height 38 cm. The binnacle has
three glazed apertures and a top glass.
Two lighting positions for the deck
candle, which is in the style of a carriage
lamp and could be used as a hand
lantern. The base of the compass houses
a tube for spare candles and a device for
locking the gimbals while in transit.
Diameter of compass card 11 cm. Liquid
compass with an expansion chamber.
Sapphire cap bearing and iridium-tipped
pivot. Beneath the lower lantern brackets
there are rings for securing the compass.
This design, Dent Patent No. 1583, was
in widespread use in England; the
example shown bears the number 51068.*

29. *Upper section of a Thomson-type
binnacle, equipped with lanterns and a
semi-circular reading glass, by W.
Ludolph, Bremerhaven. The bowl is
marked '1924 No. 384'.*

30. *Compass binnacle from the former royal yacht Victoria and Albert.*

31. *Dumoulin-Froment taximeter, around 1890. The column houses the electrical illumination. The transparent dumb-card printed on glass is set in gimbals and the sight rule is pivoted centrally. By releasing the screws on either side, the part comprising the card and bowl can be removed and the column capped off in bad weather. The lever positioned in the centre of the column operates a shade to adjust the illumination. Peloruses of this type, which were regulation equipment in the French Navy, were installed in the first large ships to be built of iron.*

CAPTAIN ARTHUR'S REGISTERING COMPASS AND THE TELEGRAPHIC COMPASS

'The main component added to the normal compass in this ingenious device is a clock-work which moves a pencil up and down a vertical cylinder, itself free to rotate about its axis. The cylinder is marked with twelve equally spaced horizontal lines, representing the twelve hours of the day or night. It also has vertical lines corresponding to all the divisions of the compass. The cylinder is set so that its North-South line coincides with the same marking on the compass. Whenever the ship deviates from its intended course a lever fixed to the top of the cylinder is pressed by one of the two inclined planes positioned in the upper part of the instrument, thus turning the cylinder either to the left or to the right and producing a corresponding pencil mark. The paper with which the cylinder is covered thus indicates both the time and the direction of deviation, in other words the course of the vessel. All the parts of the instrument are made of bronze to avoid magnetic deviation. In another proposed system the needle of the compass would be touched every minute by a special telegraphic device which would record the direction of the ship in the cabin below.' Published in the Revue maritime et coloniale, 1871.

Although no example of either of these two systems of registering compass has survived, it is interesting to read of a mechanism based on a principle that would later be used in course recorders.

32. This splendid Kelvin compass binnacle must have been a school's demonstration model. It is signed 'Sir William Thomson's patent 1876, no. 149, White – Glasgow'. Note the compensating magnets and the system for adjusting them in the column. The clinometer is missing.

The Perfecting of the Magnetic Compass

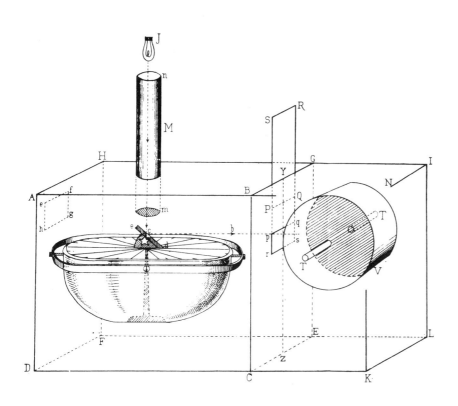

34. *The course recorder exhibited at the Brussels International Exhibition of 1897 by Edouard Bech, a navigation instructor, was an ingenious device based on the principles of photography.*

Once the heading has been set, the small mirror (or prism) fixed at the centre of the compass card is adjusted so that the beam of light from the lamp J is reflected to align with the lubber line YZ. In the right-hand compartment a drum powered by a clockwork mechanism unwinds a photographic film coated with silver bromide upon which the beam of light leaves an image. After development, the film enables the navigator not only to spy on the helmsman but also to plot the actual course on the basis of the variations in the heading followed. The following lines are to be found in the designer's description of his instrument: 'The course recorder, which keeps a watchful eye focused constantly on the compass card and provides irrefutable documentary evidence, seems destined to give valuable assistance to navigation and to increase its safety in no small degree. Its use will oblige the helmsman to steer accurately, limit course errors and the wastage of time that ensues, reduce the cost of navigation, lessen the number of shipwrecks, enable ship-owners and insurers to earn revenue and, finally, spare the vast family of mariners many senseless deaths.'

The ideas expressed in *la Mécométrie de l'aymant, ou l'art de trouver la longitude par la déclinaison* by Guillaume le Nautonnier, 1603, had not been renounced by the 19th century. Far from it, in fact, for ever since the days of Halley efforts had been made to chart isogonic lines. In 1700 Halley had published a map showing a meridian of zero variation and a change in the direction of variation, which was an innovation. He had also put forward the theory that there were four magnetic poles, two stationary and two mobile, and computed changes in variation by interpolations in time and position, which was completely wrong. It was still hoped that such magnetism charts could be used one day to obtain a geometric position, provided a compass was available that was sufficiently precise and free of deviation errors so that the variation could be measured to within one-tenth of a degree. It will be seen that this idea of networks is the same as that which was later implemented for radio navigation aids such as Decca, Loran or Toran. It was therefore believed that the magnetic compass could be perfected and the mariners of the second half of the 19th century were at pains to calculate accurately the deviation due to the ship itself. It was all the rage, and any number of 'dromoscopes' and 'dromographs' appeared for adjusting and compensating compasses without bringing up the ship. As so often happens, the magnetic compass was approaching the peak of perfection when it was superseded by an instrument based on a completely different principle that nullified centuries of research at a stroke – the gyroscopic compass.

Dromoscopes and Dromographs

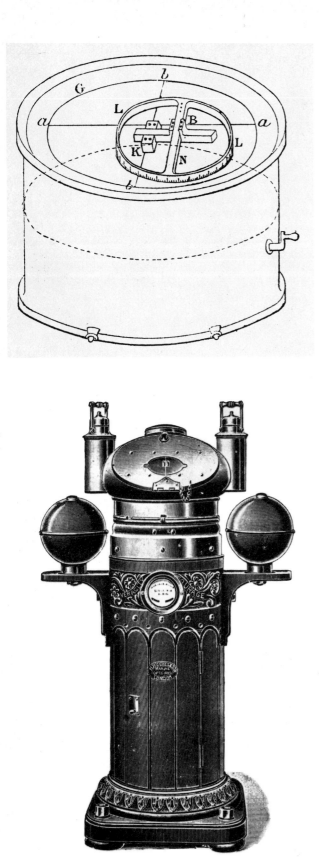

35. The following are extracts from an article by Lt.-Cdr. H. de Kérillis-Calloch that appeared in the Revue maritime et coloniale of May 1889:

'The world of science has long been deeply moved by the terrible accidents caused by ignorance of the deviation of compasses. First Poisson propounded his fine philosophical law on the working of deviation; then Smith skillfully worked it into an elegant and precise formula. However, the complicated calculations that had to be made meant that it was never used in practice and while the discovery of new laws continued apace the deviation aboard iron ships became so great that the need for compensation could no longer be ignored. On first-class battleships the needle would behave like a mad thing, surrounded as it was by massive guns, turrets and armour plating. Then along came Sir William Thomson's wonderful invention that reduced the deviation of the needle to a minimum. However, these precious advantages are of only limited value, for compensation is local and has to be completely redone upon arrival in another hemisphere. The compass has to be reswung and hence the ship must be brought up for compensation in the roadstead within sight of land.'

However, a most valuable instrument, the 'dromoscope', had just been invented by Capt. Fournier for adjusting compasses (that is to say determining the deviation curve) on the basis of only two bearings. The inventor presented his instrument as follows:

Archibald Smith's formula gives the compass deviation as $d = A + B \sin Cc + C \cos Cc + D \sin 2 Cc + E \cos 2 Cc$.

The dromoscope is an ingenious slide rule which, once set, automatically carries out all the above calculations and immediately shows the course corrected for deviation corresponding to any given compass course. It was a highly prized instrument that was used in its day with the Duchemin compass; a description of its use will be found in the periodical referred to above.

In contrast, the announcement regarding the work on the dromoscope published by Gauthier-Villars in 1885 throws light on the origin of the instrument: 'The dromoscope is an instrument that reproduces mechanically the law of compass error according to the heading of the ship. The first instrument of this kind was invented by Mr. Paugger, an officer of the Austrian Imperial Navy, and is described in Pauggers Patent Dromoscope, oder Curs Corrector, published in Trieste in 1876.'

36. An early yacht binnacle, built by the firm of Hughes.

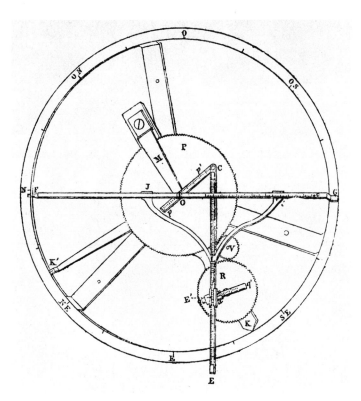

37. *Sub-Lt. Alexander Krylov of the Russian Imperial Navy, who invented a course corrector, justified the new instrument as follows: 'The complicated design of the two previous instruments (by Paugger and Fournier), the first of which is impractical and the second too theoretical, led me to construct a third.' Krylov's device, which is based on the elliptical dygograms of Capt. de Collongue, reproduces mechanically the movement described by the resultant magnetic vector, which affects the compass in accordance with the course followed. This is therefore the directive force. By using Smith's three coefficients A, B and C, d can be obtained for any heading.*

The instrument is therefore interesting since it follows the deviation.

See the Treatise on compass deviation and dygograms *by J. Belavenetz, St. Petersburg, 1872, in Russian.*

38. *The course corrector designed by Capt. Monti of Austrian Lloyd dates from 1878. In contrast to the previous instruments, it is not intended for determining the deviation curve, which is assumed to be known and plotted to a given scale in polar co-ordinates. Generally this is a rather flattened ellipse (the broken line), with the axis 0 of the instrument as the centre of the co-ordinates. If the stud/axis A is positioned over the curve, B gives the magnetic course and C automatically the compass course.*

The correction of deviation clearly depends on the shape of the track K; the inventor assumed a priori *that the deviation curve would be similar for all vessels of a particular kind, so that the instruments could be mass produced.*

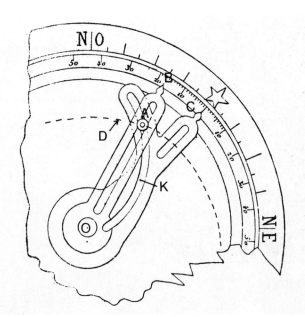

Measuring the Distance Sailed

From the Log Ship to the Patent Log

39. Streaming the log aboard the sailing ship Garthsnaid.

The development of the magnetic compass as a means of determining the direction of travel, the first component of dead reckoning, had been an arduous affair, extending from the Amalfi rose to the Thomson binnacle compass, but it took just as long to come to grips with the measurement of speed, the other element in an estimated position. The best patent logs did not appear until the end of the 19th century, only to disappear at the beginning of the 20th (in the same way as the magnetic compass gave way to the gyro-compass) when the revolutions of the propeller provided an equally good measure of the distance travelled.

Until the end of the 18th century all long passages were made by dead reckoning for want of any other method, particularly where the calculation of longitude was concerned. However, once lunar distances had been introduced, a method that did not require a chronometer, the partisans of the astronomical method fiercely attacked the age-old practices of sailors who continued to 'estimate' and were loath to use the new procedures. In his *Guide de navigation* M. Levêque had the following to say: 'At sea, compass error is seldom known with any degree of accuracy. The ignorance or carelessness of helmsmen is such that a divergence in one direction is never offset in the other. Dead reckoning is no more than a jumble of pieces, all of them wrong to varying degrees. Hence the results obtained in this way can bear no resemblance to reality unless by some miracle the errors cancel one another out, which is a severe drawback of this method. Let no-one therefore come reciting remarkable landfalls – they are nearly all apocryphal. In any case, they are so few compared with the number that are frighteningly wrong that they can carry no conviction in the eyes of an unbiased observer who knows the sea and the both clumsy and ridiculous subterfuges in which pilots indulge to lend their work an air of precision upon sighting land or indications that it is near.'

The instruments of dead reckoning: (from left to right) *small compass by Bonnet, Paris, 'Cherub' log register and rotator, protractor with moveable arm by Lerebours, Paris.*

40. *'Streaming the log ship.' While one of the sailors holds the reel high so that the line runs free, the other counts the knots as they pass and is ready to stop the line when the ship's boy calls the end of the sand-glass. On the deck can be seen a spare reel and log ship in a regulation bucket-shaped draining stand. Drawing by Morel-Fatio.*

This was all perfectly true, and no doubt it was in the distance sailed that the greatest errors occurred, especially during voyages in an East-West direction (such as the voyage of Columbus) as long as there was no means of verifying the longitude comparable to the meridian altitude of the sun used for checking distances travelled along the meridians.

The word *log* comes from the piece of wood thrown overboard at the bows and timed as it passed the length of the ship to the stern, in other words over a known distance; a rule of three gave the speed of the ship. Now let us briefly calculate a simple error. A ship making six knots covers 11,112 metres per hour, or 3.1 metres per second. On large sailing ships of the period, which measured about 35 metres, the time between the log being thrown overboard at the bows and its arrival at the stern was therefore 11.3 seconds at 6 knots. If the log was thrown too far ahead or short of the bows, or the moment at which it touched the water was badly timed, or if the ship was making leeway, or if the log was swept along by the wake or cast back by a wave, or if the moment at which it reached the stern was badly judged, the margin of error could be as large as two seconds. Two seconds more or less over a period as short as 11.3 seconds means five times two seconds per minute, or ten times the speed per second (3.1 m/s), hence 30 metres. In an hour the error amounts to 1,800 metres, or about one nautical mile. We therefore have an error of twenty-four nautical miles a day and at the end of a forty-day voyage (they were often much longer – de Grasse took ninety days to reach Chesapeake Bay from Toulon) a distance of 1,440 miles to add or subtract – nearly 3,000 kilometres! We may suppose that the errors will not all be in the same direction and will offset one another to some extent, but even half (1,500 km) is still a considerable distance. It was therefore crucial to take great care in measuring the speed.

41. Fifteen-second timer for use with the log line. This interesting device was constructed in an attempt to rid log readings of errors in judging when the sand had run through the sand-glass; this was a very difficult moment to judge, particularly at night without a lantern or in heavy weather. The instrument, which dates from the middle of the 19th century, is a kind of calibrated helter-skelter. A ball inserted through a hole at the top right as the first knot runs out rolls down five inclined planes before dropping at the bottom left into the hand of the time-keeper, who calls to the linesman to stop the line. The period of measurement was short, only fifteen seconds. Obviously the instrument will only give a true reading if it is held vertical; hence the ring-shaped suspension.

The first log to show any advance over the block of wood was described by William Bourne in *A Regiment for the Sea*, published in 1577, and was subsequently mentioned in all the treatises on navigation – Gunter's of 1623, Snellius' of 1624, Father Fournier's of 1643. It was a weighted board, the forerunner of the log ship, and the only design to have survived the ravages of time, as there was no lack of inventors if Marguet is to be believed. Quoting Vitruvius, he writes of a paddle-wheel attached to the hull which dropped a pebble into a receptacle at each revolution. In 1607 Crescentius mentions a manometer of the 'relative wind' (no doubt meaning the apparent wind), which wound in x metres of line in proportion the distance sailed.

All this presupposes, however, that there was agreement on the length of the mile and, where the log ship was concerned, the distance between knots. The first measurement, made by Richard Wright in 1589, gave the radius of the earth as 5,580 km, which was 800 km too little. Norwood measured the mile as 1,866.6 m using a surveying chain and advocated theoretical knots of 51 feet and practical knots of 50 feet in order to allow for the forward drag of the line. This was a great improvement, as until then a distance of 42 feet had been used, which according to the pilots of those days 'ensured a safe landfall', since by counting too high a speed they expected to arrive well before they would and hence would keep a look-out in time!

Practical navigation's gain was science's loss, and the men of science, represented in France by Chabert, Bouguer, Gaigneur and Radouay, protested vigorously against the pilots.

The terrestrial league was originally 'the average distance covered in one hour by a traveller on foot'. This vague measure was retained for oceanic voyages, whereas in the Mediterranean the mile was used. Columbus had

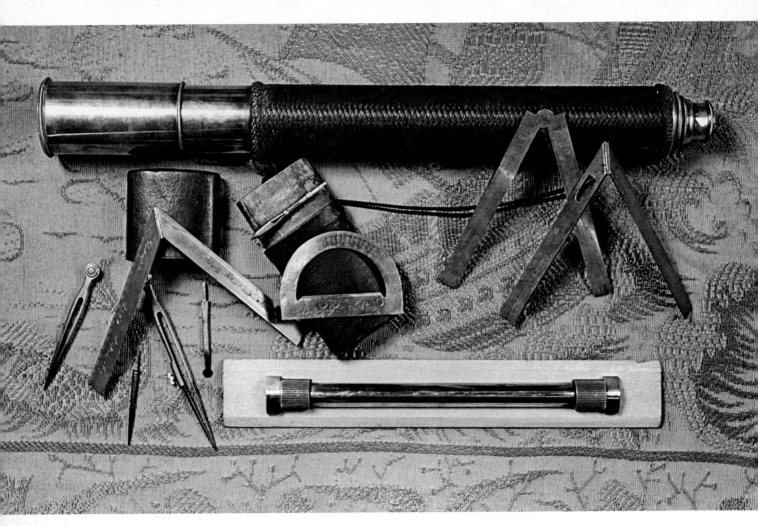

Pilotage and calculation. Top: *a French three-draw telescope with shade, covered in plaited leather.* Centre: *a set of drawing instruments by Butterfield comprising the case, a compass for lead, ink and serrated wheel, a pair of dividers, two set squares, one graduated in Rhine inches and the other in French inches, and a sector.* Bottom: *rolling rule.*

Traverse board, signed 'G. Touboulic, Brest' mid 19th century. Right up to the last days of sail, navigation by dead reckoning continued to undergo incredible refinement that went far beyond what could reasonably be expected of instrument-based estimates and even the assessment of errors. Touboulic's traverse board is one such device for refining the details required to plot the course on the chart. The central rose has nine concentric circles of holes, one for each half-hour of the watch; it is marked out in half points, thus giving the course to within 6°. Brass markers are used to indicate the course. Around the rose there is a semi-circular board, marked out for each hour of the four-hour watch and from zero to 90°, for indicating leeway! The line of holes between the two scales is used for recording compass error (variation plus deviation) from zero to 45° on either side – a generous allowance. Bottom left: *eleven lines of ten holes each are provided for recording the miles run, from zero to ten; in this respect the designer thought small, doubtless because he had never known a ship to exceed ten knots.* Bottom right: *board for marking down the ship's speed in tenths of a mile as measured with the log, in other words to the nearest half-second, which meant that the sailor responsible for the sand-glass had to have a pretty sharp eye.* Bottom centre: *a small table for indicating the helmsman's steering precision, which is recognised to be biased in one direction.* ▶

CONSTRUCTION
ET USAGE
DU SILLOMÉTRE,

INSTRUMENT nouvellement inventé, destiné à observer en Mer le sillage des Vaisseaux en dixiemes parties de lieue par heure, l'angle de la dérive à la précision d'un demi-degré, & par lequel on trouve avec la plus grande facilité la position la plus avantageuse d'un Vaisseau relativement à sa marche.

Publié sous l'Approbation de l'Académie Royale des Sciences.

INVENTÉ par M. DE GAULLE, Ingénieur de la Marine, de l'Académie Royale des Sciences, Belles-Lettres & Arts de Rouen, & Professeur d'Hydrographie au Havre, le seul chez qui on puisse se procurer cet Instrument.

M. DCC. LXXXII.

Explic.

Fig. 1.ᵉʳ Coupe de l. largeur, marque connoître le m.

Fig. 3. L'instrumen. côté qui doit être.

Fig. 2. L'instrumen. une position ver. visuels de l'observ. sur la partie i.

Fig. 4 et 5. Les pl. dans l'eau; dont Les lettres indiqu. piece servant à. Conformément à.

42. Title page of the work by De Gaulle, a naval hydrographer and inventor of a 'sillomètre' or speedometer, 1782. With great honesty the author notes that the term 'sillomètre' was first used by Chevalier de Fleurieu, a naval captain and Director of the ports and arsenals of the Realm. The name was apt, as the instrument measured the 'sillage' or 'seillage' of the ship, which in contemporary French meant its speed.

43. Plate reproduced from the designer's monograph. It will be seen that this instantaneous speed indicator is really nothing more than a dynamometer. One of the two conical weights shown on the right of the diagram was towed under water astern and offered a calibrated resistance. The device pivots on its axis, so that it also shows the angle of leeway, a useful piece of information for plotting the estimated position. A footnote to the monograph states that 'This instrument is made at Le Havre in the workshop of Monsieur Arnal, master founder, but it may be obtained only by applying to the author'.

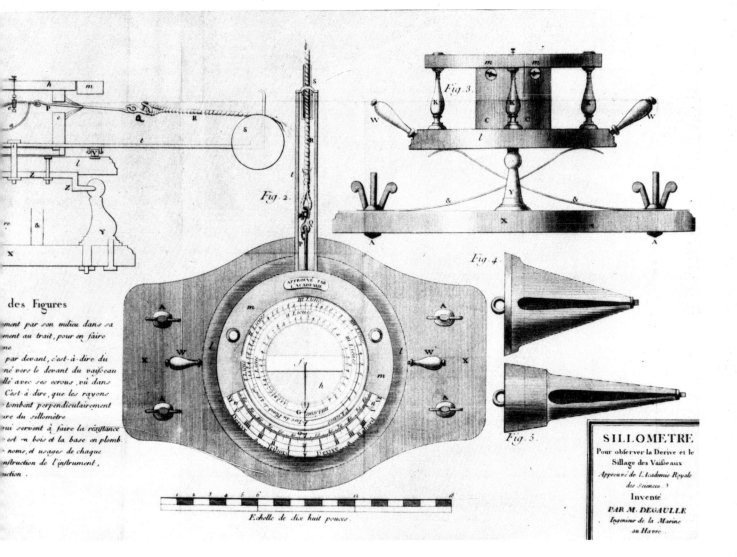

SILLOMETRE

Pour obferver la Derive et le
Sillage des Vaiffeaux

Approuvé de l'Academie Royale
des Sciences

Invente

PAR M. DEGAULLE

Ingenieur de la Marine
au Havre

Echelle de dix huit pouces.

44. In contrast to the countless devices that existed
only on paper, the speedometer designed by De
Gaulle was actually produced, probably in small
numbers, although a few examples such as the one
shown here may still be found.

Many designers tried their hand at dynamometer
logs. Bouguer suggested a regulation log consisting
of a canon ball towed astern at a certain depth; the
speed of the ship could be estimated from the angle
of the tow rope.

Small traverse board, brass on wood, more sensible for use at sea than Touboulic's sophisticated instrument. Unsigned and undated, it consists of twelve concentric roses of the thirty-two points of the compass, each rose representing a half-hour in a six-hour watch (such interminable watches were the general rule on ships with only two officers). Below the rose are four lines of ten holes each for indicating the speed in knots. They were less punctilious about the speed, which had to be measured four times a watch, in other words every hour and a half during a six-hour watch. This was a laborious task using the log ship. However, the holes at the end of the line provide for accuracy to within a quarter of a knot.

45. Foxon's hydrometer. By the King's patent, no. 43. *This instrument, which was constructed by William Foxon, a carpenter of Deptford in Kent, has a wooden case with three glazed apertures for the dials. It is one of the earliest types of recording log, having been patented in 1772. The three register dials are graduated in twelve parts, which are sub-divided decimally; each dial therefore has 120 divisions, so that elaborate hourly calculations may be made. The large wheel at the top of the instrument, the axis of which forms a direct extension of the log line, acts as a governor. The device was used with a torsion-free line about fifteen fathoms long and a very coarse-pitch helical rotator which, because of the very principle on which it was based, was bound to give dubious results, particularly in heavy weather, as was noted by James Cook, who used the instrument during his second voyage.*

counted fourteen and one-sixth leagues to the degree of longitude and eventually, at the time of Father Fournier, the great circle of the Earth at the Equator was measured as 5,400 German leagues, 6,300 Spanish leagues and 7,200 French leagues. The nautical league used by France and England, measuring one-twentieth of a degree, gained acceptance, being recognised by *Neptune français* in 1693 and adopted without modification by the French Hydrographic Department in 1720. The nautical league thus measures three miles, the mile being equivalent to one minute of latitude at the Equator. One mile equals ten cables, the cable having a length of one hundred French 'toises' or one hundred and twenty fathoms and the knot represents a speed of one nautical mile per hour.

There is little that can be said about the proposal to calibrate the worn and fast-running thirty-minute sand-glasses against the half-second pendulum defined by Le Gaigneur – a lead shot, between 7 and 9 millimetres in diameter, hung from a silk thread 24.8 centimetres long and released at a distance of between 8 and 11 centimetres from rest!

46. *Massey log, 28 cm long, patented in 1802. Engraved 'T. Massey, London'.*
Three dials – one-eighth of a mile, miles and tens of miles. Massey's final design
also recorded hundreds of miles. The inner mechanism comprises an endless screw
and toothed reduction gears, as in the later Walker logs. A cover completes the
register. The device was towed under water, held horizontal by its stabilising fins,
and had a propeller to drive the movement of the register. It remained in use in the
Navy until the middle of the 19th century.

47. Top: *register and rotator of a Massey log.* Bottom: *Gould log (Gould Patent,*
Boston, about 1800). The dials are graduated in miles, tens and hundreds of miles.
The rotator has a screw and cone so that the aperture of the blades can be adjusted
without changing the pitch in order to correct for the effects of cavitation at speed.

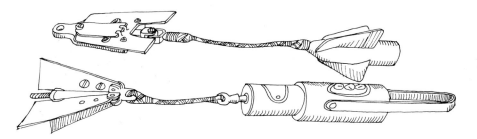

LOCHS A HÉLICES

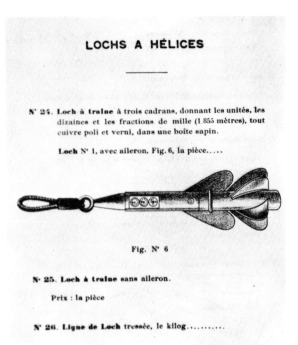

N° 24. **Loch à traîne** à trois cadrans, donnant les unités, les dizaines et les fractions de mille (1.855 mètres), tout cuivre poli et verni, dans une boîte sapin.

Loch N° 1, avec aileron, Fig. 6, la pièce.....

Fig. N° 6

N° 25. **Loch à traîne sans aileron.**

Prix : la pièce

N° 26. **Ligne de Loch** tressée, le kilog..........

N° 27. **Sabliers** 15 et 30 secondes, la pièce.......

48. *Advertisement for a retailer of hydrographic and nautical equipment. The log register is a taffrail log of the Walker variety, which was mounted in a bracket at the stern.*

49. *Page from the catalogue of a ship's chandler in Saint-Malo, about 1890. The towing log illustrated, with integral register, is the Walker model shown on the dust-jacket of this work.*

50. *The first recording log, of American manufacture but sold widely in Europe. The speed of rotation of the screw was adjusted precisely by making saw cuts in the blades.*

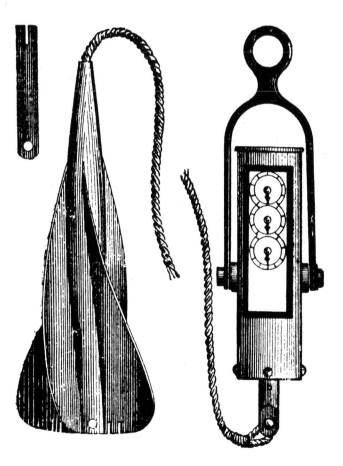

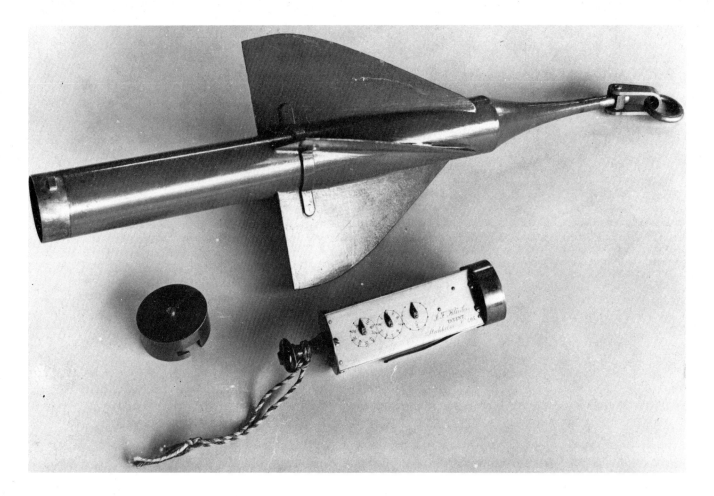

51. *Log signed 'P. F. Klinlin, Patent,*
Stockholm No. 405'. This interesting
type of log was towed astern at the end
of a rigid tow-bar. The blades turn the
movable tube containing the register, the
fixed point being the tapered forward end
of the instrument. In order to read off the
number of miles run the log had to be
hauled in and the register withdrawn.

Around 1770 Goimpy perfected the calibration of the log by calculating the factors of error – the catenary of the line and the forward drag exerted by the wake. As early as 1732 Pitot had put forward a system from which the modern pressure log was to spring and which was used by reference to a table. In 1773 Bouguer submerged the log ship to a depth of fifty feet in order to obtain the speed over the ground in the belief that currents did not run at such a depth. He then devised a second system using a submerged cannon ball which involved measuring the angle of the tow line. The system invented by the hydrographer De Gaulle, which is described in this book, was actually made in 1782; it showed only the instantaneous speed, however, as it lacked a register. The first known propeller log appears to have been designed in 1768 by Wallot, a German inventor; it included a revolution counter and was tested on *l'Enjouée*. Foxon's log dates from 1772, but it was really Massey who, in 1802, gave the impetus for a series of mechanical logs from which the Walker and Gould logs were developed.

52. *Plath log register, marked 'Sillomètre', for use with Walker's Cherub rotator. This German design, manufactured in Hamburg by the well-known firm of nautical instrument-makers, dates from 1870.*

LE PILOTE
EXPERT.
DIVISE' EN DEUX PARTIES.

LA PREMIERE Contient l'Explication des Termes de l'Art de Naviger & le moyen de trouver la moyenne Parallele de differentes façons, & ce que c'est que moyenne Parallele.

Le moyen de reduire les lieuës de Longitude en degrez par l'Echelle Angloise. Les Tables pour trouver la difference en Latitude & Longitude.

La Variation de l'Aimant. La qualité de la Pierre d'Aimant; de sa vertu inclinative des lieux où il se trouve; de sa bonté, & de son utilité.

Les Tables des Amplitudes Ortives ou Occases.

LA SECONDE Contient les Deffinitions de la Sphere. Les Ephemerides du mouvement du Soleil. Les Tables Sexagenaires; celles de sa Déclinaison, & celles de ses Ascensions droites, avec les noms des principales Etoiles du Firmament.

Le tout avec de bonnes & justes Démonstrations.

Par le Sieur DASSIE C. R.

❋❋❋

AU HAVRE DE GRACE.

Chez JACQUES GRUCHET, Imprimeur & Libraire de Monseigneur le Duc de S. Aignan, & de la Ville.

M. DC. LXXXIII.
AVEC PRIVILEGE DU ROY.

53. *Title page of the work by Dassié, Le Havre, 1683.*

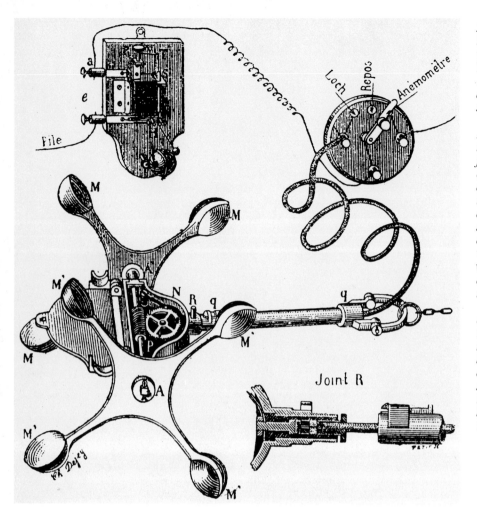

54. *Fleuriais electrical log. This instrument had a double paddlewheel and was tested aboard the battleship L'Océan in the Bay of Quiberon in June 1888. With cups twenty-five centimetres apart and making one revolution a second, the accuracy is approximately 4.85 knots < V < 4.89 knots. At speeds of more than ten knots the log is totally unreliable. The tow-line is a four-strand codline of 60 mm circumference, the electric wire being one of the strands. Sail thread seizings at intervals of one metre prevent any distortion of the wire. The mechanism is simple; a watertight box contains an endless screw driven by the cupped wheels, the screw itself turning a gear wheel equipped with a peg which makes an electrical contact once every revolution.*

The bell therefore rings once every complete revolution of the gear wheel. A table gives the speed of the ship in relation to the time between rings. It will be noticed that the inventor had thought of applying the same principle for a wind speed indicator, or anemometer, as indicated by the second position on the bell contact-maker, no doubt connected to a cupped wheel at the mast-head.

Electricity came aboard naval vessels with the early Gramme dynamos, and batteries were also used to produce small quantities of current. The Fleuriais electrical log with its cupped wheels dates from 1888. Meanwhile many systems based on pneumatic transmission or electrical impulses were developed.

The length of the mile was fixed at 1,852 metres and for those sailing ships still using a log ship and thirty-second glass the theoretical knot measured 15.43 metres and the practical knot 14.62 metres to allow for drag. Such great advances were made with the Walker-type log that it gave the speed through the water to one-twentieth of a knot. This type of log was to remain in use until just after the second world war, being used on steam-ships in addition to the number of revolutions of the screw (corrected to allow for the state of the hull) for estimating the distance run.

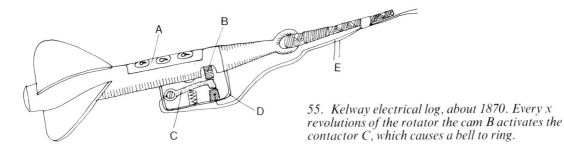

55. *Kelway electrical log, about 1870. Every x revolutions of the rotator the cam B activates the contactor C, which causes a bell to ring.*

56. *Experimental speedometer designed by Lt. V. Banaré and tested aboard the steam despatch vessel* le Corse *in 1868. The device has a screw H supported by a chassis C and a block of cork L. A piston activated by the screw via a crank-arm and rod mechanism works bellows S, thus transmitting impulses to bellows S^1, which in turn drives an integrating meter. The instrument does not seem to have been produced commercially; however, it is based on an interesting principle that was to be used in automation a century later for pneumatic control systems aboard modern ships.*

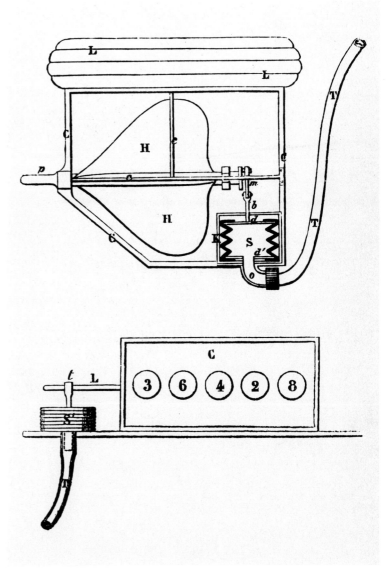

Determining the Ship's Position

The Chart and Plotting the Course

Premières Heures *by Jacques Devaulx, a pilot, Le Havre, 15th century. One face of the terrestrial globe, reflecting the geographical knowledge of the time. The 'equinoctial line' marks the Equator. It is no longer known what the carefully drawn outlines of the 'Terre des Grands Vents' (Land of High Winds), the 'Terre des Tourmentes' (Land of Torments) or the 'Gouffre Austral' (the Austral Gulf) in the southern hemisphere represent. However, as a sketch of Australia, showing the Gulf of Carpentaria, it is quite remarkable. As for the 'Terre australe incogneue' (the unknown southern land), this represented the geographers' conception of an Antartic continent that logically had to exist to counterbalance the weight of the land masses concentrated in the northern hemisphere. How the imagination is fired by such a view of the world, in which the voyager is carried by the south-west monsoon from the 'Isles Tristes' (the Melancholy Isles) around the 'Chef de bone Esperance' (the Cape of Good Hope) to 'Arabie Heureuse' (Joyous Arabia).*

The idea of depicting the Earth on a flat surface is as old as time. Countless projections have been used to do this, but nautical charts could not simply be derived from a geometric projection; they had to be based on more analytical calculations. The first nautical diagrams were the portulans. A distinction must be drawn here between rutters or pilot books, which were illustrated descriptions of the coast (called *portolanos* in the Mediterranean and *roteiros* in Portugal), and portulan charts.

The Carta Pisana, which is the oldest surviving nautical chart and is conserved at the National Library in Paris, is a portulan chart. These charts, which were constructed from innumerable small sections of flat projections, were clearly of use to sailors only over small areas. The 'marteloïo', a network of wind roses for which a standard method of plotting had been devised, was of no help in solving navigational problems, as it had no scale, no longitude and no latitude.

The problem of loxodromes, or rhumb lines, was one of the major difficulties of navigation, no less troublesome than that of longitude. By definition a loxodrome is the course that the ship follows automatically (without wishing to, so to speak) by maintaining a constant compass heading in relation to the meridians. Such a course, which is neither a small nor a great circle of the globe (an orthodrome), can only be represented on a Mercator chart. The Flemish geographer Gerhard Kremer, called Mercator, published his first map in 1569. This was derived from the globe he had produced in 1541, on which the loxodromes were more or less correct even though they had been plotted by approximation.

The Mercator chart is the true nautical chart; in France it was long called the *carte réduite* or 'reduced chart', not because it was small or covered a limited area of the globe but because of its usefulness in resolving diagrammatically, or reducing, the elements of the course – the north-southing (difference in latitude) and east-westing (difference in longitude) – which were arrived at using the mariner's quadrant. We must not forget Pedro Nuñez, a professor of mathematics in Coimbra, who expounded the basic principles of loxodromes before Mercator's time. Tribute should also be paid to Edward Wright who, following in the wake of Mercator, established the ratio between degrees of latitude and longitude governing the expansion of each point along the meridian. With remarkable patience, Wright calculated the length of the mile for each minute of latitude from 0 to 89° 59'.

Before the days of Mercator, however, and for many years afterwards, two systems of representation coexisted in addition to the portulan charts based on courses and distances. First there were *plane charts*, representations of a small portion of the globe in which a section of the sphere could be taken to be a flat map. As these charts did not show true angles, they could only be used for navigation within very narrow confines. The first plane chart to be marked with degrees of latitude, which also showed degrees of longitude and parallels of latitude (albeit equidistant), was Portuguese and dates from 1485. Charts based on *courses and altitudes* appeared later, and showed only parallels of latitude. Provided the course and the latitude were correct, the longitude could therefore be found.

In 1640 the Flemish began to print charts, eliminating copying errors and making this navigational aid readily available by virtue of the low cost and the number produced. It was at this time that protractors – described by Father Fournier as 'movable roses of bronze or transparent horn' – and parallel rulers began to appear. Stevin, the Flemish physicist who coined the

Ici est la figure de lautre moitie du globe terrestre par laquelle est demonstré les terres qui sont esleuez sur lhorison de ceulx qui habitent mesmes en l'aequinoctial qui qut les deux polles en leur horison assauoir larticque & latarticque & qui sont eslongez en oposite & point contraire des habitans de la precedente figure ci deuant, asscauoir de 90 degrez loin du grand meridien fixe en la partie orientalle dicelluy, ou aparoit les terres de l'heurope africque & asie. & c.

Par ceste presente figure est demonstré toutes les terres qui sõt cacheez desoubz lhorison de lautre figure ci deuant & aussi par mesme moyen est entendu que les terres de lautre dicte figure sont ausi chasez desoubz lhorison de ceste presente figure de maniere que l'une desdictes figures démonstre tout ce qui doibt estre esleué desus lhorison du point du milieu & lautre figure démonstre ce qui doibt estre chasé desoubz

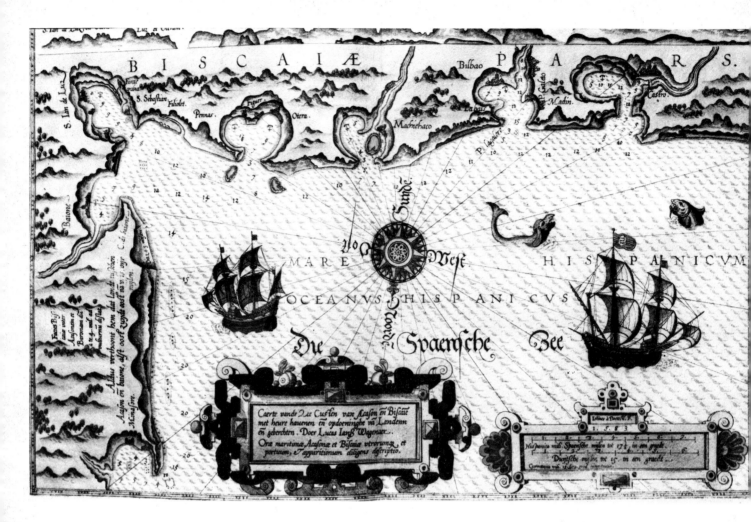

57. *Extract from the Atlas of 1583 by Lucas Jansz Wagenaer, showing the Bay of Biscay from the Arcachon basin to Bilbao. The ports of Bayonne and Saint-Jean-de-Luz can be seen in the top left-hand corner. Some profiles of the coast are shown at the top of the chart. A small number of soundings in fathoms are given. Banks and recommended anchorages are also indicated. The frame in the bottom right-hand corner shows the scale in Spanish and Dutch miles. The chart has no latitude or longitude scale. In keeping with the practice of the time, the chart is very ornate and as the outline of the land framing the chart fits the rectangular format, the compass rose in points notation has been aligned with the layout of the chart, with North at the bottom.*

terms loxodrome and orthodrome, devised improved set-squares for plotting these complicated courses on the chart and on the globe. As most of the charts were now drawn to Mercator's projection, the sinical or mariner's quadrant tended to fall into disuse.

The formula for expanding the latitude scale was to be improved in 1772 in order to make allowance for the flattening of the Earth towards the poles. At around the end of the 18th century the relief of the land began to be shown on nautical charts so that the coast could be recognised when sailing within sight of land and towards the beginning of the 19th century some uniformity seemed to be emerging in the signs and symbols used by the various hydrographic departments. However, there was still a long way to go before all the world would have been charted, so that the hydrographic departments shared the task of surveying. This was to last until 1880 as far as the most frequented regions were concerned. In 1920 there was still plenty to be done, checking details, filling in gaps and, above all, correcting longitudes, which were often inaccurate. In 1722 Marguet gave examples of huge errors in the charts supplied by the Navy's cartographic office for the Cape of Good Hope, a much visited area. As for Cape Horn, at that period its co-ordinates were given as 61° 36′W, 51° 5′S instead of 67° 30′W, 55° 43′S. It is now known that the shipwreck of the *Méduse* was caused by an error of more than 30′ in the longitude of the Belin chart. Many such errors in longitude, which were appreciable before the days of chronometers, still had to be eliminated; some have remained even to this day in the charts of the Hydrographic Department, although the doubtful areas are marked.

58. The Sea-mans Practice, *by Richard Norwood, 1644.*
*The work includes a detachable cut-out diagram, as was
common at the time. In 1622 Norwood was sent to
Bermuda on a hydrographic expedition; between 1633 and
1635 he measured the distance between London and York
with a surveying chain in order to determine the length of
one degree along a meridian. His measurement, which was
the first of its kind to be carried out in England, was 600
yards out, but nonetheless consistent with the instruments
available. Norwood's main concern was the length of the
nautical mile, which he estimated at 2,040 yards, or 12
yards too much. It was Norwood who gave 51 feet as the
distance between knots on the log line used with a half-
minute sand-glass. He is also attributed with having
discovered the dip of the compass needle as early as 1576.*

THE
SEA-MANS
PRACTICE,
Contayning
A FVNDAMENTALL
PROBLEME in Navigation,
experimentally verified :

Namely,
*Touching the Compaſſe of the Earth and Sea, and the
quantity of a Degree in our Engliſh meaſures.*
ALSO,
An exact Method or forme of keeping a reckoning
at Sea, in any kinde or manner of Sayling.

With certaine Tables and other Rules uſefull in Navigation. As alſo in the Plotting and Surveying of places.

The Latitude of the principall Places in ENGLAND.

The finding of Currents at Sea ; and what allowance is
to be given in reſpect of them.

By RICHARD NORWOOD, Reader of the
Mathematicks.

LONDON,
Printed by T. FORCET for *George Hurlock*, and are be ſold
at his Shop neere St. *Magnus* Church. 1644.

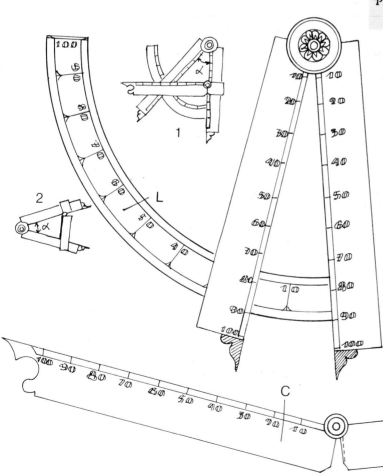

59. *The sector invented by Thomas Hood in
1598. The forerunner of the slide rule and the
calculating machine, the sector was used in
solving trigonometric problems
diagrammatically. The angle between the two
arms is set by means of the arc L. The cursor C
is then used to form the right-angle of the
triangle for ascertaining the values of sines,
cosines and tangents (fig. 1); alternatively, by
hinging the cursor so that it cuts both arms at
the same length, the value of the cord can be
obtained (fig. 2). The pointed ends of the
sector also have their uses. Contemporary
advertisements for Hood's sector state that
These instruments are wrought in brasse by
Elias Allen dwelling without Tempel barre
over against St. Clements Church: and in
wood by John Thompson dwelling in
Hosiar lane.*

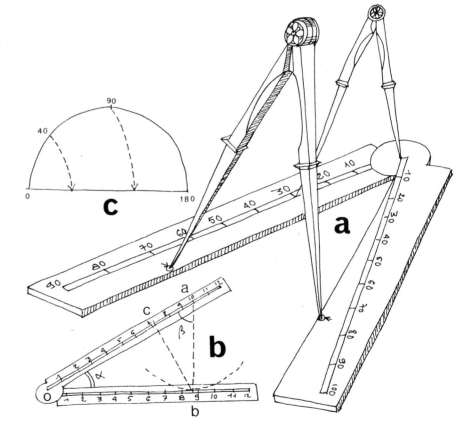

60. *Extract from the* Encyclopédie, *1767: 'Sector. Upper figure, or face 1: the divisions along the edge are inches; along the internal angle the divisions on the upper limb are degrees and those on the lower limb the corresponding measurement in grades. The divisions along the external angle are the equal parts. Face 2: the markings are used for measuring with the dividers the length required for opening the limbs of the sector to the corresponding angles.'*

61. *The use of the sector in practice. The sector must be used in conjunction with a pair of dividers. The first operation is to 'set the angle' (fig. a). Depending on the convention adopted by the designer, the scales show either lines of angles in degrees or grades (as in the diagram) or lines of cords. First the length representing, say, 30° is measured along the line of degrees with the dividers; this length is then set between the specially marked points on the sector. The sector thus forms an angle of 30° and can be used for solving all trigonometric problems involving the right-angled triangle with angles of 30°, 60° and 90°. In figure b the lines of equal parts or lines of lines are being used; these are marked from 0 to 10 or from 0 to 12, each part being sub-divided into decimals.*

Placing the point of the dividers on point 10 (a in the diagram), a circle is drawn with the corresponding line of the other limb as a tangent. The length ab represents cos β or sin ∝. ab multiplied by itself becomes $(ab)^2 = ac$, which determines point c precisely. As $cb = ab \times \sin \propto$, which we already know, we can find point b accurately; furthermore $Ob = Oa \times \cos \propto$, giving cos ∝ and tan ∝. Figure c shows cords plotted on a diameter.

60

*Wooden traverse board, German, beginning of the
19th century. Apart from serving as a reminder of
courses and speeds, the smaller traverse boards could
be used as actual protractors, the straight edge
acting as a rule and the other side of the angle being
formed by a thread attached at the centre.*

Mariners' Quadrants

Before the general publication of Mercator charts in the middle of the 17th century the only way in which the navigator could solve the problems of dead reckoning was to calculate the differences in latitude and longitude. As diagrams or graphic aids were preferred to books (traverse tables), the *mariner's quadrant* and the *nautical square* came into being.

'The mariner's quadrant is a very simple and very accurate instrument for resolving the courses steered and distances run by vessels at sea and until now no method has been found to be quicker or more accurate than that based on the mariner's quadrant which, as I shall describe, is used by applying the middle latitude.' This is the view expressed by Blondel Saint-Aubin in his work entitled *Le véritable art de naviguer par le quartier de réduction, avec lequel on peut réduire les courses de vaisseaux en mer, et enrichi de plusieurs raretés qui n'ont pas encore été découvertes.*

The formula g = e × sec Lm, which gives the difference in longitude in accordance with the east-westing and the middle latitude, came into use as early as 1623, when it was proposed by Gunter. The mariner's quadrant was still very much alive in 1768, even though Norwood's traverse tables had already become available.

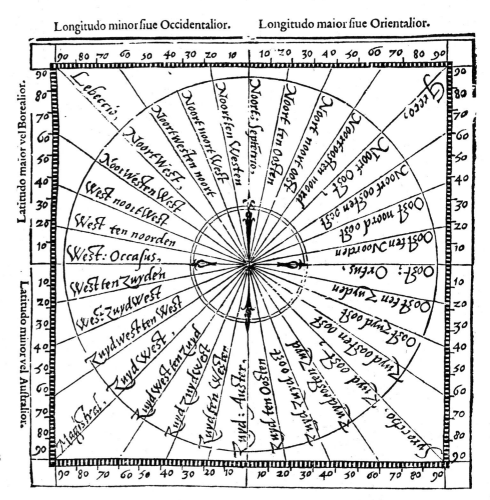

62. Nautical square by Gemma Frisius. A similar quadrant, termed a shipman's *or* mariner's quadrant, *can be found in Blundeville's work of 1636.*

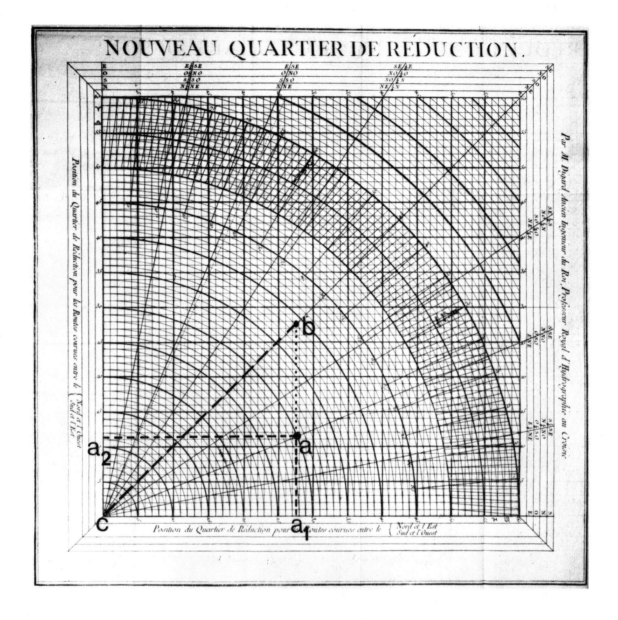

NOUVEAU QUARTIER DE RÉDUCTION.

63. *New mariner's quadrant, reproduced from* Nouvelle Pratique abrégée de pilotage, *by Kerguelle. This mathematical aid, which was either printed or engraved on metal, wood, horn or sometimes simply vellum or paper, was in common use on ships from the 17th century onwards for obtaining the estimated position diagrammatically. Nowadays traverse tables are used for this.*

It consists of: 1. A square divided into a grid of equidistant lines for transferring right-angled co-ordinates; divisions from 0 to 60, with multiples of five marked by heavier lines. 2. A network of concentric arcs centred on the bottom left-hand corner, one for each

division; multiples of five in heavier lines. 3. From the same point of origin a series of rhumbs spaced at intervals of $11\frac{1}{4}°$, in other words eight per quarter circle and thirty-two to the compass rose, with their equivalents in points notation – e.g. ESE, NNE, etc. 4. The outermost part is a scale divided into degrees from 0 to 90 and a grid of diagonals for working to fractions of a degree.

All the problems of dead reckoning could be resolved by means of this one diagrammatic instrument. Let us take an example: a ship has run 30' to the ENE and is at point a on the chart. The diagram is taken to be a plane chart with the bottom left-hand corner as the point of departure, so that the east-westing

and north-southing are the axes of the horizontal and vertical co-ordinates; e = 27.7' and l = 11.5'. In order to find g we have to plot on the graph

$$g = e × \sec Lm.$$

If Lm, the middle latitude, is 45°, say, the vertical line is extended from a to point b and the distance cb is read off as 39.2'. The quadrant can obviously be used for the other three quarters of the circle as well, so that work on the sea chart was prepared on this position diagram.

*Gimballed steering compass by Joannes van Keulen,
Amsterdam, 18th century. The card is printed from a
copperplate engraving and coloured by hand.*

Nautical Works

For centuries reading and writing were not the favourite occupation of navigators. Right up to the 19th century illiteracy was widespread among fishermen, coastal sailors and even deep-sea mariners. It is therefore easy to understand why graphic aids such as diagrams, rulers or drawing instruments met with such great success and relegated the printed word to second place.

The first rutters to be printed, and hence to be readily available, were Dutch and date from the beginning of the 17th century. Their popularity with seamen was due to the many diagrams of ports, anchorages and coastal outlines that they contained. They were in fact pilot books.

Pure navigational works, that is to say tables, appeared very early. They were intended primarily for astronomers, such as the *Alphonsine Tables* published in 1252 under Alphonso the Wise of Castile, which gave the declination of the sun. In 1475 came the *Ephemerides* of Regiomontanus,

64. One of those instruments in which the 16th century abounded. This object of both scientific and astrological curiosity is a sundial, a slide rule and a measuring instrument rolled into one. The way in which it was used is far from clear, bearing in mind the esoteric sound of the strange terms 'globes of feathers' and 'globes of iron'.

65. 'At the double helm of a three-
decker', drawing by Morel-Fatio, around
1840. Note the regulation steering
compass of the period and the helmsman
observing the heading in order to mark it
on the traverse board, the sailor's
traditional reminder.

followed by the Portuguese *regimentos*. In France the nautical almanac was
first published in 1679 under the title *Connaissance des temps*, but the
Annuaire des marées, or tide tables, did not appear until 1839. Until then the
circular pocket calculator was used. The Dutch handbook by Wagenaer
(middle of the 16th century) was considerably amplified and reproduced in
England from 1588 onwards under the title of *Waggoner*, an incom-
prehensible literal translation of the type that also produced *regiment* from
Regiomontanus. The British *Nautical Almanac* dates from 1767.

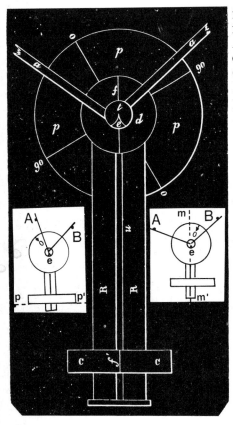

66. An ingenious instrument for working
on the chart invented by Cdr. Serval in
1872.
    The usual method of finding the
position from bearings is to correct the
angles for variation and deviation and
then plot them on the chart with
protractors. This 'graphical operator'
simplifies and shortens the process. First
the graduated circle is orientated to
correct for deviation and variation. Then
the arms a are set to the bearings Zc read
from the compass for the two objects in
question. The bar CC is placed on a
parallel and run along it while R is slid in
or out as required until the two arms pass
through the points observed. The ship's
position is then marked at the tip of
pointer e. Left-hand inset: alignment
with a parallel pp'. Right-hand inset:
alignment with a meridian mm'.

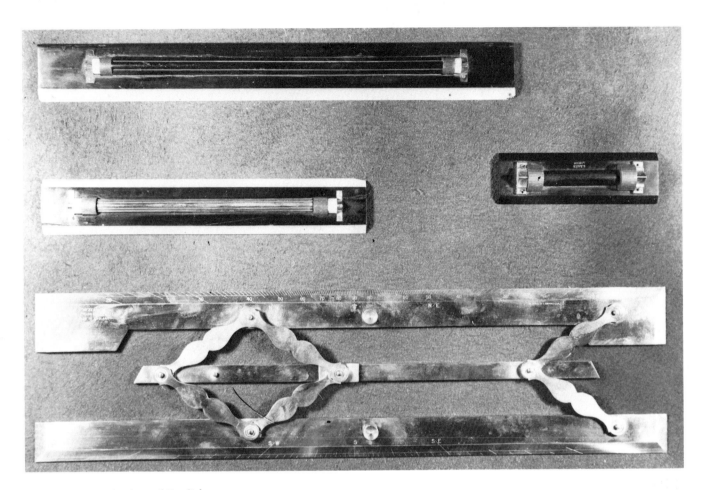

67. *Four parallel rulers of English manufacture. The three upper examples of various sizes employ the roller system and are made of ebony. The bottom rule is a Hezzanith model with a double expansion, polished brass, end of the 19th century.*

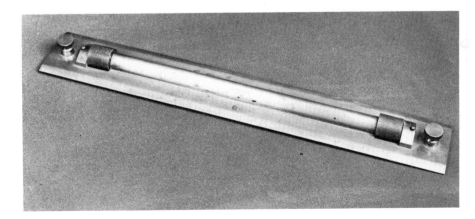

68. *Large rolling rule, 50 cm, brass, signed 'Astonmanda', end of the 19th century.*

2 · Practical Pilotage

The Pilot's Art

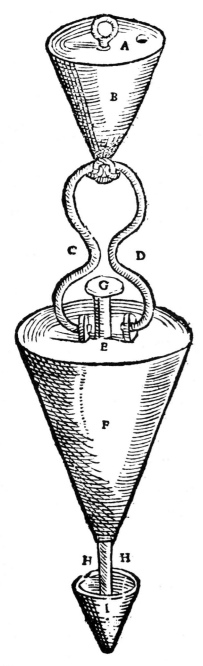

The concept of pilotage has changed over the centuries. From the early days of deep-sea sailing right up to the 18th century the pilot was the actual navigator of the vessel. The expedition was under the command of the general and the handling of the ship was the responsibility of the officers, but the conduct of navigation was the exclusive preserve of the pilot. This was true, for example in the case of Pinzón, Columbus' pilot.

In the 18th century the standard of education of officers improved with the introduction of the first certificates. Celestial navigation and dead reckoning were henceforth carried out by the ship's officers and pilotage assumed the more restricted sense of guiding the ship close to land. The pilot was a practical inshore seaman who had a perfect knowledge of the depths, channels and dangers in a limited area. Henceforth the pilot's task therefore consisted in guiding ships towards the harbours by means of the sounding lead and landmarks on the coast. The form of instruments used for pilotage has no doubt changed, but the principle of depths and transits has remained the same even though nowadays we use echo sounders, high-power binoculars or radio navigation bearings.

69. *Here is a remarkable instrument for measuring depths described in the work entitled the* Cosmolabe *by Jacques Besson, 1567. Let us first hear what the author has to say: 'To measure the depth of the sea in any place without a line, in calm weather, as accurately as with the lead-line if it was of such a length to reach the bottom of the sea ... And these two principles are proven, as heavy objects by their nature sink and light ones rise in an element to which they are alien ... Finally, the shape of the device by which the depth of the sea may be measured in any place or profundity without a line ... There will remain only one problem to resolve, viz. that heavy objects descend faster to the centre of the world than towards the circumference and light objects travel more quickly towards the circumference than towards the centre.'*

AB is the light element, EF the weight. I is a cone attached to piston H and plunger G. The whole instrument is thrown overboard and sinks. When it touches bottom, I foremost, G pushes C and D apart, releasing AB, which immediately floats to the surface. Hence, if a clepsydra (water-clock) was set in motion when the depth finder was released the time when the float breaks surface can be noted. The 'profundity' is obtained from a table as a function of the elapsed time. The combined descent and ascent time are calibrated, so that there is no need to know when the depth finder touches bottom. The only drawbacks: the need for a calm sea, the impossibility of measuring the time accurately with the sand-glasses of the period and the consumption of weights lost at each sounding.

The very modern design of the instrument nevertheless comes as a surprise, bearing in mind that it was invented in 1567.

Taking Soundings

One of the first principles of navigation being to keep water under the keel, pilots naturally hit on the idea of measuring the depth of the water either to discover whether the bottom shelved at the approach to an unknown coast or to find their position by reference to a depth line in an area that had already been surveyed.

The stone weight on the early sounding lines was soon replaced by lead, which was heavy and compact. The obvious unit of measurement was the *fathom*, which was the length of line brought up at each pull by a natural movement of the arms. Until the 19th century only primitive hand leads were used. The deep-sea lead-line consisted of a line of more than 20 fathoms attached to a lead of between 18 and 25 pounds, a considerable weight to cast and retrieve, while the small lead for depths of less than 20 fathoms had a weight of between 5 and 7 pounds.

70. The sounding fly invented by Edward Massey at the very beginning of the 19th century is well known. It consists of a very long lead weight (truncated in the photograph) and a counter. The device is set at zero and dropped overboard. The rotator drives the scale, graduated in fathoms, by means of an endless screw until the sounder touches bottom. While the instrument is being retrieved the pressure of the water depresses the upper disc, thus locking the rotator. It will be seen that it is not necessary to feel the instrument touch bottom; if allowed to fall freely, it will record the depth as it descends and lock automatically as it is hauled in. Accuracy depends on the free movement of the gears, hence on their cleanness and lubrication.

71. This variation on the principle of the Massey sounding fly was made by Duchemin, a clockmaker in Saint-Malo, around 1850. The instrument is allowed to fall freely and the scale, which has previously been set to zero, converts the revolutions of the rotator into fathoms. The horizontal vane locks the counter as the device is hauled in.

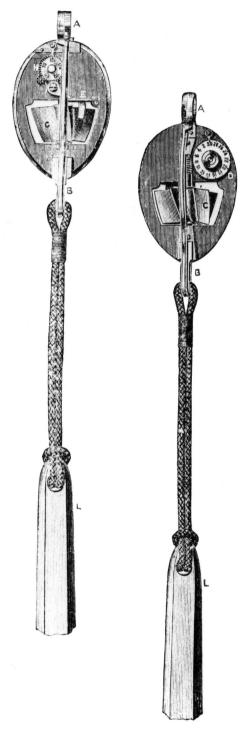

72. *Walker's improved depth sounder based on the Massey system. It has two dials, one calibrated from 10 to 30 fathoms, the other from 30 to 150, a kind of integrating meter that records five times as many revolutions as the first. The endless screw is driven by the propellor. When the lead touches bottom it frees the propellor locking device; the depth is thus measured as the instrument is hauled in.*

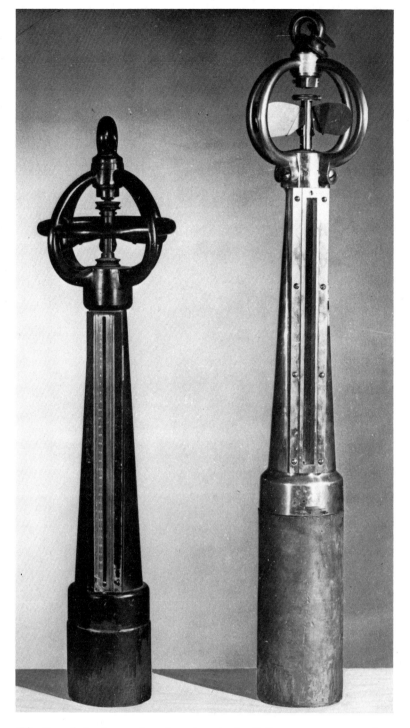

73. *French depth sounders, based on the Le Coëntre system, around 1843; the example on the left was made by the instrument maker Dufresne. The propellor works during the ascent, not on the way down. As the cursor is at the limit of its travel the mechanism can only operate as it is being hauled in. The depth is given by the position of the cursor against the longitudinal scale.*

74. *Using the deep-sea lead-line. This was a tricky operation, even with the way off the ship, because of currents (which could cause a marked slant in the line), the weight of the lead (between 15 and 20 kgs.) and the weight of the line, not to mention the difficulty in feeling the seabed at a depth of 150 m when it was of soft mud. Woodcut from a drawing by Morel-Fatio.*

LA PRATIQUE
DU
PILOTAGE.
OU
SUITE DES ELÉMENS
DE PILOTAGE.

Par le P. PEZENAS, de la Compagnie de JESUS, Professeur Royal d'Hydrographie à Marseille.

A AVIGNON,
Chez FRANÇOIS GIRARD
Imprimeur & Libraire.

M. DCC. XLI.

75. *Title page of the work by Father Pezenas, Director of the Marseilles Observatory. Avignon, 1761.*

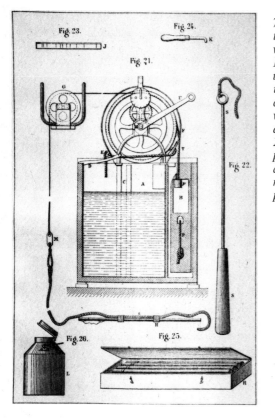

76. *Thomson sounding machine. With this instrument soundings of depths up to 100 fathoms could be taken while under way at a speed of up to 15 knots. It was designed, in fact, more with hydrographers in mind than merchant seamen. Nevertheless, up to thirty years ago a fair number of merchant vessels were still using it to take very precise soundings on the approach to land in areas with unusual seabed contours. The principle behind it is simple: a coating of silver chromate on the inside surface of a glass barometric tube is discoloured by water as it rises inside the tube in proportion to the pressure exerted by the depth. The cable carries a very heavy lead (fig. 22) and a brass tube holder (fig. 25). The glass tubes could be used only once. An iron hook (fig. 24) is used to pluck the wire cable in order to ascertain whether the lead has touched bottom and the sounder should be raised. The moment when the bottom is reached is of no significance, however, as the angle of the line does not affect the indication of pressure.*

With the development of mechanical logs there also appeared ingenious systems for measuring the depth by the number of revolutions of a rotator recorded on a counter. These were followed by systems based on hydrostatic pressure. The final step was the invention of piezo-electric sounders, quartz sounders (using ultrasonic frequencies) and sonar sounders.

It was in the age of hand leads that seamen showed themselves most adept in the art of making a landfall by soundings thanks to the contour lines on the chart. The interpolation of soundings was an everyday procedure and any number of methods were taught in schools of hydrography. This was, after all, the only safe method in fog when approaching the coast of Europe, sailing around Iceland or along the American seaboard.

77. *Advertisement of about 1910 for the Warluzel depth sounder. The advantages extolled defy comment. This too was a full-size machine for installation on large vessels. The interesting feature of this particular sounder is that the measuring tube could be used repeatedly.*

To See Afar in Order to Foresee

78. Two-draw telescope, made by or for Jacob Cunigham, 17th century. Pasteboard and leather.

If 'to navigate is to foresee', as the well-known aphorism goes, then the ability to see a long distance greatly increases the margin of safety by allowing manoeuvres to be anticipated, whether in order to avoid a natural danger or to flee a possible enemy. For this reason extending telescopes were adopted by seafarers as soon as they were invented.

The early instruments, however, had inherent drawbacks for the seaman. In order to obtain a large enough image it was necessary to increase the length of the telescope and thus reduce the field of vision, which made observations impossible when there was a swell running. Moreover, below a certain focal length lenses suffered from such chromatic aberrations that they were unusable. When Dollond discovered how to manufacture achromatic refracting systems in the middle of the 18th century, optics took a great leap forward. It was now possible to use lenses with a short focal length and obtain a large magnification. The production of perfectly polished lenses was another major problem in optics that was not resolved until the end of the 18th century. Early telescopes were made of pasteboard and leather, then wooden tubes were used and finally brass draw-tubes. On board ship the telescope came to be called 'the glass'. The eye-piece of an

79. Large six-draw telescope of the Semitecolo type.

80. *Various nautical and travelling telescopes.* Top: *wooden and brass telescopes.* Bottom: *three-draw Semitecolo telescope.* Left: *telescope bound in shark-skin, by Watkins, London.* Centre: *small travelling telescope.*

81. *An interesting example of fancywork in plaited cotton on a ship's telescope.*

ordinary telescope consists of four lenses – two to erect the image and two to complete the achromatism. The magnification depends on the focal lengths of the five lenses and the distances between them. Black-painted rings called dividing plates are placed between the lenses in order to block off dispersed light that would otherwise blur the image. The magnification is the apparent increase in the size of the object viewed. The field of vision is defined as the angle subtended by an object filling the field as viewed by the naked eye. The intensity of the light is the image brightness and the sharpness of the image is called the definition.

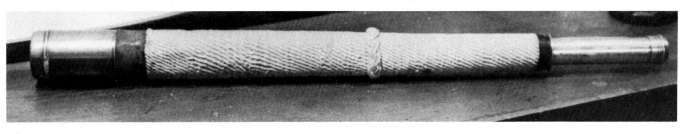

82. *Drum-reading micrometer by Admiral Fleuriais. The circumference of the eye-piece is marked with equivalences of angles and distances. The final model of this instrument, made by P. Ponthus, successor to L. Petit, Paris, had an accessory with two concentric scales, a kind of circular slide rule. The instrument-maker defined its use as follows: 'When the linear height of an object is set against the index, its distance is indicated opposite the angular height in minutes.'*

Other instruments were given the same name even though they were based on different principles:

'The micrometer is an optical instrument in the form of a medium-sized telescope; it is also called a prismatic telescope on account of the prism that constitutes the main component of the system within the instrument. It measures small angles with sufficient accuracy to give the distance from one ship to another within acceptable limits for artillery fire. It was invented by Rochon and perfected by Arago.

The frigate on which gunners are trained for naval service makes constant use of the instrument, and it is to be desired that this practice should spread. . . . In surveying it is used for measuring base-lines across water where the surveying chain cannot be employed.'

83. *An octant converted into a micrometer by the addition of a toothed arc and a large vernier of thirty divisions. The index arm is signed H. Hacke, Neukölln, 6930, and bears the registration number M. 1640.*

3 · Celestial Navigation

The determination of position on the surface of the globe by the observation of celestial bodies is one of the greatest achievements of science. One can well imagine the time that passed between passively observing the motion of the stars and using this immense sidereal clock for the purposes of navigation. This too required measuring instruments and an appropriate method.

The laws on the movement of celestial bodies were the result of work carried out by the Dane Tycho Brahe (1546–1601), the German Johannes Kepler (1571–1630) and the Englishman Sir Isaac Newton (1642–1727). Up until then astronomy had not progressed beyond the stage of simple observations using the sun or the pole star. It was also Newton who stimulated the development of modern observation instruments, as we shall see later.

The ancients discovered that the pole star was more or less stationary in the celestial vault and so navigators would hold a course in relation to this fixed star or stay in the same latitude by applying the principle of equal altitudes of observation. The sun was more elusive, with its seasonal variation in declination, but it too was mastered once the laws it obeyed were known. There can be no doubt that from the early centuries of the Christian era onwards astronomers used the sun for calculating latitudes and determining the North-South axis of the meridian. If the historians of the Pacific are to be believed, the islanders made their long voyages partly by dead reckoning and partly by the direct observation of the stars in season, obtaining the latitude by observing the exact angle of reflection of sunlight passing through holes pierced in the top of a gourd and reflected from water in the bottom.

Cosmographers' early endeavours revolved around the physical realisation of the position triangle, in other words the exact three-dimensional construction based on the angles between the pole, the star and the zenith. If it is reconstructed on the globe, this triangle should determine the exact position of the observer. The idea was logical, although rather naive in view of the relative scales involved, and it was only because of the imprecision when applying the method to a small globe that it was abandoned in favour of calculating the components separately from precise observations – the altitude to within a minute of arc and time to the second. It must be remembered, however, that the world was just emerging from an era in which alchemy held sway, with its philosopher's stone and esoteric sciences; this fresh perception by direct observation was in itself a great advance over the 'logical' preconceived ideas about the world.

Spheres

Spheres and globes occupy an important place in the early history of navigation. Not knowing how to represent the Earth on a flat chart for nautical purposes, navigators used globes and dividers for calculating real courses and distances. The first known globe, which is now conserved in the Germanisches National-Museum, was constructed in 1492 by Martin Behaim upon his return from Portugal. It is made of pasteboard covered with vellum and measures 51 cm in diameter. Asia is shown so close to Europe that one is inclined to believe that Columbus would have been tempted by such a short crossing.

At about the same time, 1520, appeared Schoener's world chart and in 1540 that of Mercator. The coming of the Mercator chart in no way hampered the production of globes, which gave expression to the contemporary knowledge of the world and simplified the assessment of distances on long voyages.

Besides such globes made up of printed gores, which were published from 1600 onwards, navigators used blank spheres, celestial globes and, of course, armillary spheres showing either the system of the world or the local celestial sphere for making rough calculations.

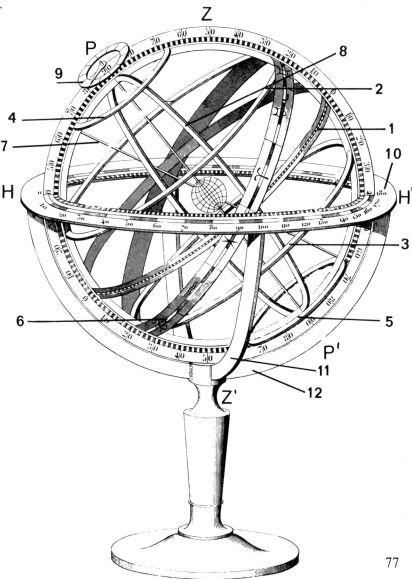

84. The armillary sphere is a physical representation of the local celestial sphere, the Earth being at the centre of the system. The instrument is better suited for college and school demonstrations than for calculations and in principle relates only to the sun, the course (or ecliptic) of which is shown.

The base supports a cradle which represents the horizontal co-ordinates and embraces all the equatorial lines. HH', number 10 in the figure, is the horizontal plane, the scale indicating the azimuths of the sun from 0 to 180°. Nunber 12 is the meridian plane passing through the zenith Z and the pole. 11 is the prime vertical. The equatorial co-ordinate's are represented by the network of great and small circles. Number 8, or PZP'Z' the great meridian circle. 1 is the Equator, 2 the Tropic of Cancer, 3 the Tropic of Capricorn, 4 the Artic Circle, 5 the Antarctic Circle, 6 the ecliptic and 7 the axis of the ecliptic. The mobile meridian, represented by the pointer travelling over the dial 9, indicates angles at the pole. On the Earth, positioned in the centre of the instrument, are shown meridians, the Equator and parallels of latitude.

The Cosmolabe

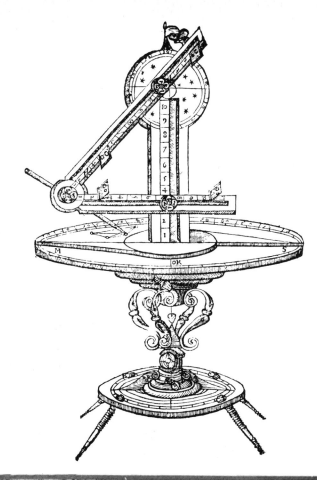

85, 86, 87. 'The "cosmolabe", or universal instrument for all observations that may be made by mathematical science, be it in the heavens, on land or at sea. Invented by Monsieur Jacques Besson, teacher of the said sciences in the town of Orleans, 1567.'

This forerunner of the theodolite and the star globe expresses well the preoccupations of the scientific world in the middle of the 16th century, absorbed by astronomy and mechanics and seeking to square the circle by developing an instrument that could solve diagrammatically the great problem of a position on the globe on the basis of direct observations of the stars or, closer to home, the determination of time by direct observation. The instrument – in this instance a 'cosmograph' – has a plumb-line for making perpendicular adjustments, sighting pinnules, graduations for measuring altitudes and azimuths and a plotting pantograph. Another view of the cosmolabe with an interchangeable platform is shown on the facing page. The science of cosmography expounded in the treatise on the cosmolabe did not spread to practical navigation, for it could not pass the formidable test posed by the author's proposal for a gimballed observation chair – another cherished illusion – which is pictured on the facing page: above.

89. *Trade card of the famous English instrument-maker Thomas Tutell. Note the illustrations of various mathematical and nautical instruments, some well known, others less so. Curiously, the last few lines of the card are written in French, no doubt for advertising in France, where English equipment was highly regarded.*

88. *Four-armed dividers for taking measurements on the globe.*

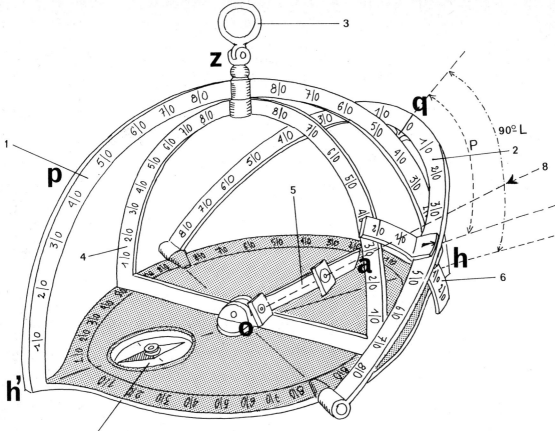

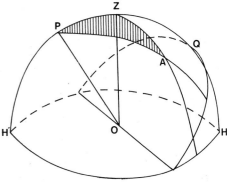

90. *Nautical hemisphere by Michel Coignet, 1581. This instrument, which has features of both the armillary sphere and the star globe, was an interesting though impractical attempt at determining the time by direct measurement. It had already come a long way compared with the cosmolabe shown on the preceding pages. Using the various components of the hemisphere the position triangle can be reconstructed from the observable elements (altitude* h *and azimuth* z*) and the computable element (declination* D*, obtained from tables), so that the polar angle* P *can be obtained. This is how it is used: The instrument is hung by the ring (3), thus causing the plate to adopt a horizontal attitude, and oriented in the meridian plane (semi-circle 1) by means of the compass (7). The azimuth semi-circle (4) and the sighting arm (5) are then adjusted until the sight vanes point to the sun in the same way as with an astrolabe, the image of the first pinhole falling on the second giving the direction of the sun (8). As the solar declination for the day is known, the graduation on the azimuth semi-circle (indicated by the alidade) can be aligned with the value of* D *set on the small arc (6) by adjusting first the angle of inclination of the equator semi-circle (2) and secondly the position of 6 on the equator by means of the slide. It is then simply a matter of reading off on the equator semi-circle the polar angle* P *between the meridian plane and the position of the declination arc. The colatitude on the meridian circle is* 90° − L*, hence we can find the latitude* L.

The small letters p, z *and* a *have been indicated on Coignet's hemisphere in order to evoke* P, Z *and* A*, the conventional letters representing the position triangle shown in the adjacent diagram. It will be seen that the sides of this triangle have the following values:* ZA = 90° − *altitude,* PZ = 90° − *latitude and* PA = 90° − *declination and that the angles are* P̂ = *polar angle,* Ẑ = *azimuth and* Â = *angle to the sun.*

Two 18th-century planetaria or orreries, wood and paper. The sun is placed at the centre of the system and the Earth is shown with its satellite – the moon – on a separate arm. The two rings serve as reference points. The ecliptic is marked with the signs of the zodiac. In the foreground: a small 18th-century celestial globe, along the lines of the later star globes.

Taking the Altitude

Early Instruments for Measuring Angles

91. Using the astrolabe for indirect sights (by the shadow cast) as shown in Arte de navegar *by Pedro de Medina. As the instrument was heavy, an assistant was in fact needed to orientate it in the meridian plane (altitude of culmination) and above all to take a precise reading once the alidade had been set.*

The idea of calculating latitude by measuring the altitude of a celestial body, in other words the angle between the horizon and the star in the meridian plane, was first put into practice by observers on land. For them it was easy to measure the angle of culmination at the moment of transit by using an instrument with a meridian plane and a sight arm.

It was a different matter on a heaving deck at sea, where the meridian plane was poorly defined and the observer had to sight the horizon and the star at the same time. The Arabs, who sailed up and down latitude in the Indian Ocean, had a measuring instrument called the *kamal*. This was a square of wood threaded on a knotted cord. If the board was held up so that the sun was sighted at the upper edge and the horizon at the lower, the board was at a precisely determined distance from the eye. This was where the knotted cord came in; each knot represented an angle in tens of degrees and any angles between these had to be found by interpolation. Accuracy was another matter, but the principle was nevertheless interesting. It was in fact no different from the principle behind the staff that Europeans held at arm's length to measure altitude or the area of a piece of ground, the rudimentary instrument that spawned the Jacob's staff described in the *Traité de trigonométrie* by Levi ben Gerson of Avignon in 1342. This was a surveying instrument that also went under the names of forestaff or cross-staff.

When did seafarers appropriate the instrument? Probably at the very end of the 15th century when celestial navigation was in its infancy, but it seems to have enjoyed immediate popularity because it was light, practical and precise. Forward observations, which were difficult because of glare, were superseded by backward observations, that is by the shadow cast. The cross-staff had several cross pieces or transoms, in some cases as many as four,

92. Title page of the important work by Pedro de Medina: Regimento de navegacion, *Seville, 1563. This, the author's second work, was dedicated to Philip II, King of Spain and of the New World.*

This would seem an appropriate point for a comment on the terms regimento *in Spanish and* regiment *in English, which are absolutely meaningless in themselves. They are in fact phonetic translations of 'Regiomontanus', which is itself a Latin translation of Königsberg and the surname given, in accordance with the custom of the time, to Johann Müller, the German astronomer, who was born in Unfind near Königsberg in 1436. According to Delambre, he was the greatest astronomer that Europe had produced until the sixteenth century. It was the title of his main work – Johannis Regiomontani de Triangulis Planis et Sphericis . . . – that led to the ambiguous use of the common word* regiment *to describe an important work on any subject.*

82

The Mariner's Astrolabe

93. *Mariner's astrolabe.*

each used in conjunction with a separate set of graduations on the square-section staff. In 1768 the Jacob's staff was still in use, as these lines from the chapter entitled 'Of the instruments appropriate for observing the altitude of the pole' in a contemporary treatise on navigation prove: 'These instruments are the cross-staff, the back-staff and the octant. All three are equally good when the weather is calm and the sun bright, provided the corrections appropriate to each are made, namely the apparent semi-diameter of the sun of 16′, the height of the observer's eye above the sea, ordinarily between 12 and 15 feet on a ship, which gives a 4′ dip of the horizon, and the atmospheric refraction that must be taken into account when the sun is less than 45° above the horizon. The table is to be found in the *Instruction des pilotes*, in the one dealing with the height above sea level, together with the method for making these corrections.

'When a back observation is taken with the cross-staff it is the upper limb

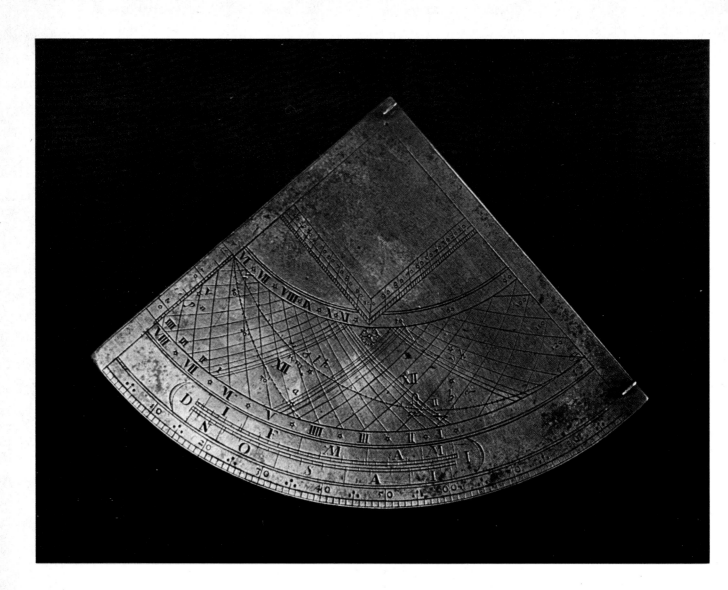

Gunter quadrant, unsigned, about 1700, probably English. On the front: two pinnules for taking sights of stars. The plumb line is missing. Along the limb is a scale from 0 to 90° for measuring altitudes, at the top is the shadow square and in the space between is a projection of the celestial sphere, with the positions of five major stars marked.

of the sun that casts the shadow of the transom on the end piece. Hence, the number of degrees read on the staff for the distance of the sun from the zenith must be increased by 16′ for the semi-diameter of the sun.

'The difficulty with this kind of observation is that since the square end of the staff must be put to the eye it is not possible to position the centre of the eye precisely at the centre of the staff nor to glimpse simultaneously the horizon at one end of the transom and the star at the other. For this reason the lowest stars should be chosen in order to bring these two points close together so that the eye has a smaller change to make to see both within the shortest interval possible.'

The astrolabe, which is made out to be the first observation instrument used by seamen, seems to have usurped its reputation. It was invented by the Arabs, initially for taking terrestial observations, but was later simplified in the extreme – stripped of its tympans and *rete*, the projection of the sky for the place of observation – so that it was no more than a graduated circle fitted with an alidade. It was made heavy so that it would hang vertically by its own weight. Using the cast shadow method the altitude of the sun could be measured to within half a degree, but with the rolling of the ship the altitude of stars sighted direct was taken to within 4 or 5°. Old hands with the

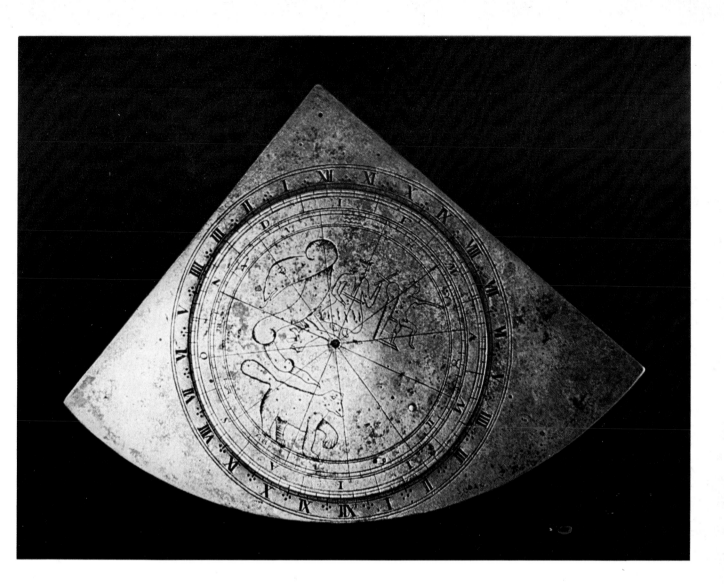

astrolabe claimed to be able to make more precise observations and had nothing but contempt for those who used the cross-staff, calling them *star shooters* in an allusion to the cross bow; however, the cross-staff gave an angle to within 12′ or 15′, which was very good.

Various modifications of the cross-staff were put forward, first by Gemma Frisius, who designed a cross-piece sliding on the staff but made the tip adjustable as well. In 1753 Bouguer the Younger suggested that for 'backwards' observations a large fixed transom could be used, with only the end piece sliding on the staff.

In the meantime another instrument based on the determination of the vertical had appeared – the Gunter quadrant. This was a quarter circle in wood or metal with two pinhole sights along one radius. As soon as the star appears in the sights the plumb line is pressed against the arcuate scale and the zenith distance can be read off directly. Accuracy is to within 1 or 2 degrees. For greater precision a large diameter instrument would be necessary, but this would be heavy and would catch the wind. However, both the astrolabe and the Gunter quadrant had the advantage that they eliminated the need to correct for dip, which caused so much controversy, Father Fournier believing it to be zero and others exaggerating it.

On the reverse: the two scales, one movable and showing the twelve months of the year and the other fixed and marked with a double graduation to twelve hours, suggest that this may be a nocturnal system using one side of the right angle as a polar axis.

94. *Mariner's astrolabe, by J. Renaud, Marseilles, 1800. A simple model with sighting pinnules.*

The Gunter Quadrant

95. *Gunter quadrant by John Prujean, Oxford, about 1680. Constructed in accordance with the principles laid down by Edmund Gunter in 1623, this quadrant offers the seaman two sighting pinnules, a scale from 0 to 90° and a plumb line for taking the altitude of stars. It is also an astronomic instrument, however, with a stereographic projection of the sky (Equator, ecliptic, Tropic of Cancer and the positions of five stars). This example, which was made for the latitude of Oxford, also has a shadow square and a zodiacal calendar.*

The Cross-staff

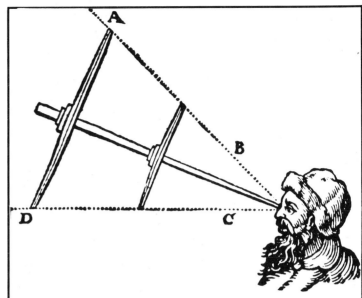

96. *The original use of the cross-staff for taking direct sights. DC is the horizon line and AB the line of sight to the sun. ABCD is the instrumental altitude.*

97. *A sensible use for back observations. The observer's eye is no longer bothered by glare nor tired by attempts to look at the sun and the horizon simultaneously. The back-staff has a special perforated cross-piece fitted at the end of the staff so that the horizon and the shadow cast by the main cross can be seen at the same time.*

98. *Reproduced from* Cosmographia *by Apianus and Frisius. The 'Jacob's staff', an old instrument for measuring angles, was adopted by astronomers for measuring angular distances between stars and was soon being used at sea.*

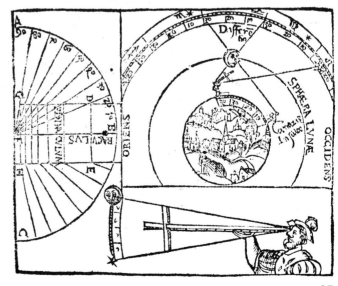

The following arguments in favour of the star globe are to be found in La navisphère, instrument nautique. Instructions pour son usage *by Cdr. H. de Magnac, 1881:*

'It can be used to find quickly, by mechanical means, the names of the stars above the horizon at any given time and their azimuths and altitudes to within one degree.

It allows stars to be identified from their observed altitude and azimuth.

It can also be used to determine the course, to within one degree, needed to travel from one point to another along a great circle arc, and the distance between the two points to within 15'.

Another application is in ascertaining the variation of the compass at time T shown on the deck watch, set to apparent time at solar noon.

The system of arcs of a circle that completes the star globe is called a metrosphere.'

Carried away by his own enthusiasm, the inventor gives odd examples of how the instrument may be used: 'Lack of attention to the course can lead to a loss of 5 miles a day [at least!]. Calculations have been made with regard to the Mexico run, from Saint-Nazaire to Veracruz. For a steamer this is a round trip of 42 days, so that, at a rate of 5 miles per day, the loss amounts to 210 miles by the end of the voyage, or 19 hours steaming at 11 knots. If the steamer consumes 43.7 tons of coal per hour, giving an additional expense of 1,529 francs per trip, the total cost over 24 voyages in a year comes to 36,696 francs, to which must be added operating expenses for the time in question. All in all the cost will therefore be at least double, that is 73,400 francs.' The inventor states that the star globe can also be used for working out variation. Compass bearings of five or six stars are taken for a given sidereal time. The star globe is set to this time, the correct bearings are read and the difference between the two sets gives the variation.

The booklet indicates that in 1879 the star globe was being produced by Eichens, the builder of the Paris Observatory, at 77 rue Denfert-Rochereau.

A French educational star globe, 48 cm high, external diameter 28 cm, made about 1880. Instruments of this kind were used in naval colleges for demonstration purposes. At the foot is a small liquid compass called a 'dory compass', which was being produced in Nantes to the original design until 1939.

The Back-staff

The back-staff or Davis quadrant, the development of which can be traced through the pages of this book, was the first truly nautical instrument and was produced in great numbers, although very few examples have survived. This is what was said of it in 1768, several decades after the invention of the octant:

'The back-staff has taken the place of the cross-staff, not because it is more accurate, but because when the sky is overcast the lens concentrates the ray from the centre of the sun just as soon as its reflected image can be seen on the octant. The cross-piece bearing this lens is set at one of the angle markings on the side of the small arc according to whether the sun is high or low above the horizon. There is another graduation on the back of the same arc for the *shadow vane*, which is used when the sky is clear and the sun bright. This vane is also set against the scale, which corrects for the semi-diameter of the sun as it is its upper limb that casts the shadow, as with the cross-staff. Although this instrument has an advantage over the cross-staff on account of the lens, it cannot be used for observing the altitude of stars.'

Of course, the serious drawback with all these instruments was that observations were difficult to take. This was even true of the Davis quadrant, in spite of the fact that the eye had to sight only one object, as the image cast by the sun on the vane was brought into line with the direct sight of the horizon. As we shall see, many arrangements of pinnules and graduated arcs were tried, some more ingenious than others. Nonetheless, reflecting instruments and pivoting mirrors opened a new era in celestial navigation by introducing a degree of accuracy that had never been attained before. By the end of the 18th century the octant had supplanted the back-staff for ever.

99. From The seaman's secrets *by Capt. John Davis, 1595. An early version of the back-staff for measuring angles up to a maximum of 45°. It is in fact an improved Jacob's staff, the curved cross-piece being slid along the staff until its shadow falls on the vane at the end of the staff. There is no pinnule attached to the cross.*

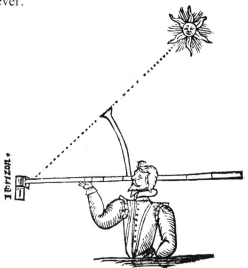

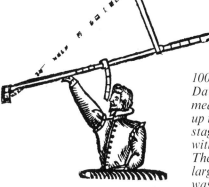

100. The second stage of the back-staff, or Davis quadrant. The larger cross could measure angles up to 60°, the smaller one up to 30°. This was still an intermediate stage in the evolution of the back-staff with two fixed arcs fitted with pinnules. The angle was first set roughly on the large cross-piece and final adjustment was made on the small one. The angle measured was the sum of the two angles inscribed on the limb, the graduations being calculated in terms of the trigonometric tangents of the angles.

QVATRIEME LIVRE

DE LA HAVTEVR DV SOLEIL,
ET COMMENT ON SE DOIT GOV-
VERNER PAR LVY EN LA NAVIGATION.

101. *From* L'Art de naviguer, *a French translation of the work by Pedro de Medina.*

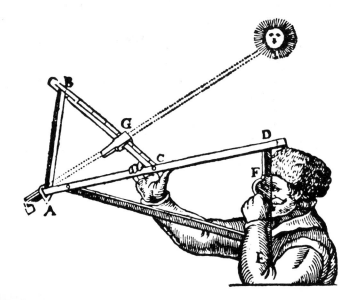

102. *A back-staff or Davis quadrant.*

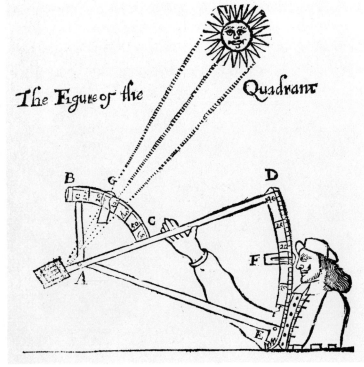

103. *The third and final stage of the back-staff. Halley and Flamsteed replaced the shadow vane by a magnifying glass or 'burning glass' (G). The widest angle that could be measured was 90°.*

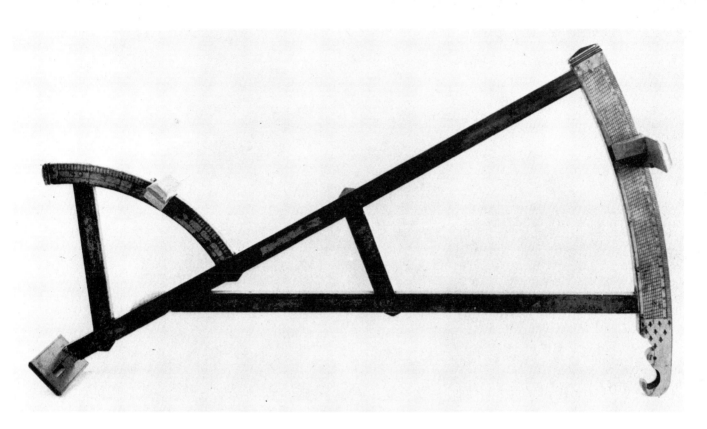

104. *Backstaff, complete with vanes. Unsigned and undated, but very probably English.*

A nevv and neceſſarie

Treatiſe of Nauigation containing *all the chiefeſt principles*
of that Arte.

Lately collected out of the beſt Mo-
derne writers thereof by M. Blundeuile , and by him
reduced into ſuch a plaine and orderly forme of
teaching as euery man of a meane capacitie
may eaſily vnderſtand the ſame:

They that goe downe to the Sea in ſhips, and occupie their
buſineſſe in great waters: Theſe men ſee the workes of the
Lord and his wonders in the deepe. Pſalme, 107.

105. *Title page of the work by T. Blundeville: 'M. Blundeville, his exercice, containing eight treatises . . . verie necessarie to be read and learned of all young gentlemen that have bene exercised in such disciplines, and yet are desirous to have knowledge as well in cosmographie, astronomie and geographie, as also in the arte of navigation, in which arte it is impossible to profite without the helpe of these, or such like instructions.*

The second edition corrected and augmented by the author. With the volvelles printed on one folding leaf, 5 separate tables or maps, and many illustrations and diagrams.'

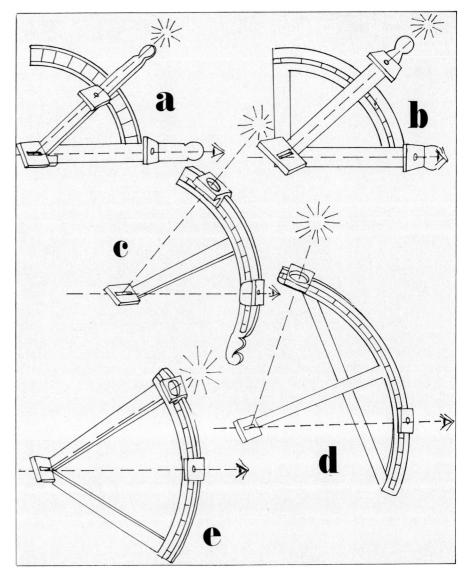

106. *Variations on the theme of the sector: (a) nautical quadrant mentioned by Pedro de Medina; (b) nautical quadrant of about 1604; (c) a simple arc with a pinnule, described by Wright in* Certain errors, *1610; (d) Edmund Gunter's 'crossbow', 1623; (e) simplification of the Davis quadrant by Bouguer. In this instance the two sectors have the same radius. The lens is fixed and only the pin-hole sight is movable. It may be recalled that Bouguer was the first to devise acceptable formulae of refraction.*

Reflecting Instruments

There are conflicting theories about the origin of the octant, so that it is necessary to present here the evidence on which they are based. The *Philosophical Transactions* record that in May 1731 John Hadley presented a paper to the Royal Society in London accompanied by two instruments, one in wood with three mirrors and the other in copper. The latter was tested aboard the yacht *Chatham*.

Upon the death of Edmund Halley in 1742, however, a manuscript by Sir Isaac Newton came to light among his papers describing 'an Instrument for observing the Moon's Distance from the Fixt Stars at Sea', which was supposed to have been presented to the Royal Society in 1699. Dr. Hooke also has claim to the paternity of an instrument of this type that was said to have been found at the Berlin Observatory in 1749 (see the *Abhandlungen der königlich preussischen Akademie der Wissenschaften zu Berlin*). The instruments designed by Caleb Smith and Elton were also known.

Hadley's quadrant was tested at sea in 1732 by the Astronomer Royal, James Bradley. In 1757 Capt. Campbell of the Royal Navy suggested increasing the scope of the octant to 120°, thus creating the sextant. There were innumerable later modifications, perfections and sometimes even retrograde steps.

With the large 50 cm Hadley quadrant accuracy is of the order of one minute of arc on the diagonal scale (leaving aside scale errors and eccentricity). It should be remembered that the first vernier to be fitted to a Hadley quadrant was divided into twenty parts. A booklet describing the instrument published by Le Maire the Younger in Paris contains, under the title 'New English Quadrant', the delightful statement that 'The instrument is so precise that attention must be paid to refraction'. Under the critical scrutiny of scientific mariners the remaining imperfections of the octant were gradually ironed out by the precise evaluation of the errors involved. Prismaticity of the index mirror was a source of major error, followed closely by eccentricity and inaccurate graduation. Marguet very rightly comments that 'The sextant is an ingenious instrument in that the errors

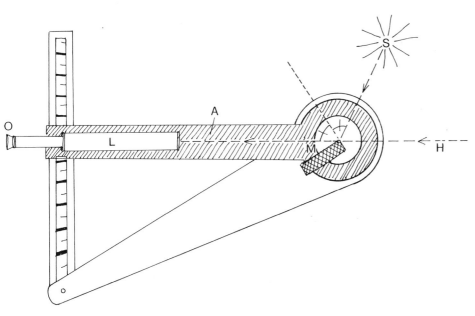

107. In 1666 Robert Hooke described an instrument of his invention to the Royal Society in London. It had a single mirror and this was probably the first time that anyone had thought of using a pivoted mirror to measure altitudes. However, the mirror is not used to the best effect, as the fundamental property of a system of two mirrors is that once the two images have been brought into contact they remain together, even if the instrument is moved. It is therefore probable that this instrument was never tried at sea and that the principle behind it was forgotten when Hadley produced his octant. According to C. H. Cotter, the instrument in question is an iron quadrant mentioned in the Abhandlungen der königlich preussischen Akademie der Wissenschaften zu Berlin *for 1749. But is this really Hooke's instrument? Levêque also refers to it in his* Guide du navigateur *of 1779.*

108. *Sir Isaac Newton tried to improve the nautical quadrant. He seems to have been the first to suggest using two mirrors, an idea that was later adopted by Hadley. Newton's idea lay dormant for fifteen years and was not mentioned again until Edmund Halley revived it on his own account. By then, however, Hadley had already perfected his quadrant. The sketch is self-explanatory: the horizon can be sighted direct through the small half-mirror M', while the large mirror M is pivoted. For a given rotation of the mirror the image moves through twice the angle, so that the scale is graduated to twice the actual value.*

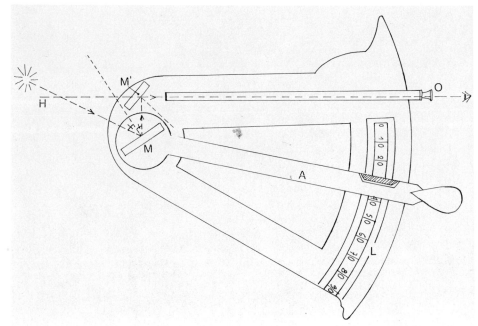

109. *Is it conceivable that inventors are unaware of each other to this extent? Whatever the truth of the matter, the Baradelles (Jean-Louis-Jacques, 1752–1794, or Nicolas-Eloi, 1774–1814), well-known makers of scientific instruments, produced this octant based on precisely the same principle as that of Newton and Halley with the unabashed inscription on the limb 'Inventé par Baradelle, Quay de l'Horloge du Palais, à l'enseigne de l'Observatoire'. It will be observed that with the telescope bearing on the large mirror direct, this instrument is a simple Hooke quadrant.*

110. *John Hadley (1682–1744) presented two types of reflecting instrument at the meeting of the Royal Society held in London on 13th May 1731. The first, which was very similar to Halley's instrument (*right*), was made of wood and had mirrors of polished brass. As these tarnished rapidly they were replaced by glasses silver-plated on the face in order to avoid prismatic errors, good mirrors being rare in those days. Simultaneously Caleb Smith designed a measuring instrument based on the same principle but using prisms instead of mirrors (*see the following page).*

*The second design (*below*) is very close to the final octant. It is made of brass and the telescope is on the opposite side of the frame compared with the normal octants that were later produced commercially. A screen is fitted above the index mirror. This large octant can also be used for back observations, for which the telescope is placed in position O, with coloured shade W and cross-wires Q for sighting the horizon. The tests on this second octant were carried out aboard the yacht* Chatham *on 30th and 31st August and 1st September 1732.*

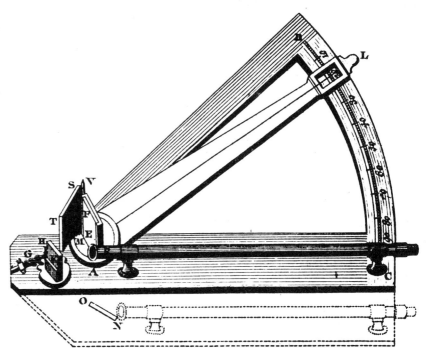

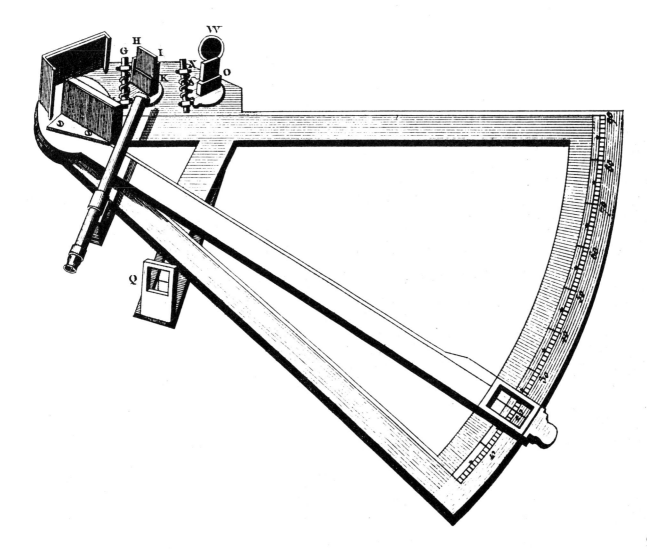

111. The principle of Caleb Smith's octant, as described by Pezenas and Rochon. The smaller mirror is replaced by a total reflection prism P with angles of 44° at the apex and 68° at the base. The instrument is held in the position shown in the figure, the observer sighting downwards. The index arm A alters the position of the large mirror M, which is adjusted to zero by means of the perpetual screw R before the observation is taken.

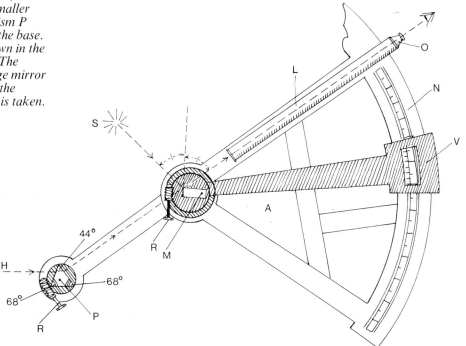

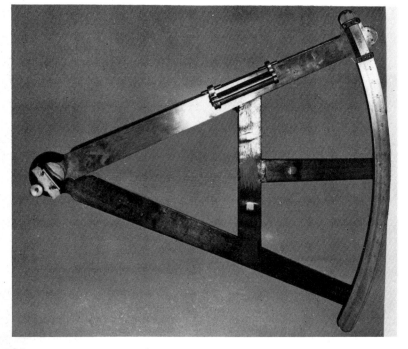

112. The octant produced by Bird, a London instrument-maker, is a late design to Hooke's principle with a single mirror. Very soon after making this first model Bird was producing sophisticated Hadley quadrants.

Large ebony octant, 50 cm radius, with a pin-hole sight and two small mirrors for forward and back observations. The attachment for the coloured shades is missing. Graduation of the arcuate scale by the system of so-called diagonals. Unsigned, about 1750.

resulting from imperfect correction are minor in comparison with those caused by the inherent irregularities of the instrument.' The remaining development of the octant, the sextant and the quintant during the 19th and 20th centuries depended solely on the instrument-makers. The multitude of shapes sprang from the method of construction that each maker considered best to ensure the rigidity of the frame – single, double, solid, perforated, reinforced – adjustment of the mirrors and lenses, the accuracy of readings by means of verniers – initially flat but later drum reading – a variety of coloured shades and eyepiece shades, the appropriate size of instrument – large and sophisticated for large vessels, small and simple for fishermen, pocket sextants for surveyors, double sextants to increase the angular range, hydrographic quintants for measuring horizontal angles – and so on.

The illustrations in this book can only hint at the almost limitless range of variations produced.

113. In 1732 Thomas Godfrey, a glazier in Philadelphia, gave details of an instrument he had invented to the Royal Society in London, which awarded him a prize of £200. The principle of the instrument is simple: the horizon is sighted direct through the telescope and the image of the sun is reflected from the front surface of the large mirror onto the horizon glass.

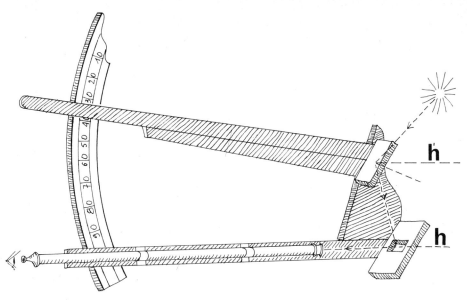

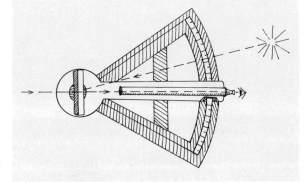

115. The first instrument made by Fouchy, Secretary of the Royal Academy of Science in Paris, in 1732 was a return to first principles. The horizon was sighted through the telescope mounted on the index arm, which was held horizontal, the large mirror being fixed to the frame. The observation was taken with one's back to the sun.

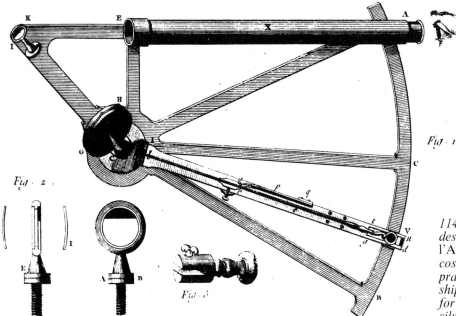

114. Fouchy's second instrument, described in the Mémoires de l'Académie of 1740, was a delicate and costly device, more scientific than practical, and was never used aboard ship although it was originally designed for navigation. The large mirror was a silvered planoconvex lens.

116. Instruction des pilotes, *by Le Cordier, 1748.*

INSTRUCTION
DES PILOTES,
OU TRAITÉ DES LATITUDES,
SECONDE PARTIE,

QUI CONTIENT TOUT CE QUI EST nécessaire pour observer exactement la Latitude, ou la hauteur du Pole dans tous les lieux du Monde, tant aux Etoiles qu'au Soleil.

Avec les Tables de leur Déclinaison & Ascension droite, & celle de la Latitude & Longitude d'un grand nombre de Lieux.

Par feu M. Le Cordier, Hydrographe du Roi.

DERNIERE EDITION,

Revüë & corrigée par J. Le Cordier, *Prestre; aussi Hydrographe du Roy à Dieppe.*

AU HAVRE DE GRACE,
Chez la Veuve de Guillaume Gruchet & Pierre Faure, Imprimeur & Marchand Libraire.

M. DCC. XLVIII.
AVEC PRIVILEGE DU ROY.

LE GUIDE
DU
NAVIGATEUR,
OU
TRAITÉ DE LA PRATIQUE
DES OBSERVATIONS
Et des Calculs nécessaires au Navigateur.

Orné de Figures en taille douce.

Par M. LEVÉQUE, *Correspondant de l'Académie Royale de Marine, & Professeur Royal en Hydrographie & en Mathématiques à Nantes.*

Le Trident de Neptune est le sceptre du monde.
Le Mierre.

A NANTES,
Chez DESPILLY, Libraire, haute grande-rue, près de celle de Beau-Soleil.

M. DCC. LXXIX.
Avec Approbation & Privilége du Roi.

117. Le Guide du navigateur, *by Lévêque, Nantes, 1779.*

99

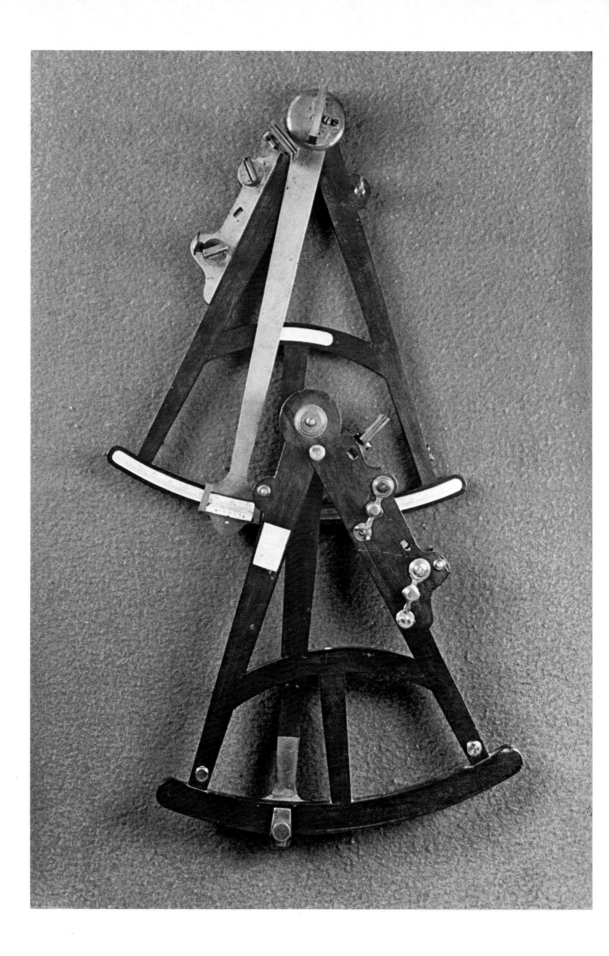

Top: *sextant by Jecker;* right: *octant by Joseph Roux, Marseilles;* bottom: *the first sextant by Lorieux.*

Two ebony octants equipped with a vernier and two small mirrors for direct and back observations. The system of coloured glass shades, which could be removed and fitted in the lower hole, can be seen very clearly. Non-prismatic shades were rare as they were difficult to make, and it may be assumed that these instruments had a single interchangeable set.

On the lower instrument, which has been turned round to show the reverse, the two cams for adjusting the mirrors to scale zero can be seen on the right-hand side. The vernier clamping screw is visible on the limb. The white inset on the left-hand arm of the frame is an ivory or bone plaque for noting the measurement in pencil. The pencil, which is missing in this example, was a lead held in a small cylinder of turned ivory which fitted into a hole in the central cross-member (visible in the lower instrument).

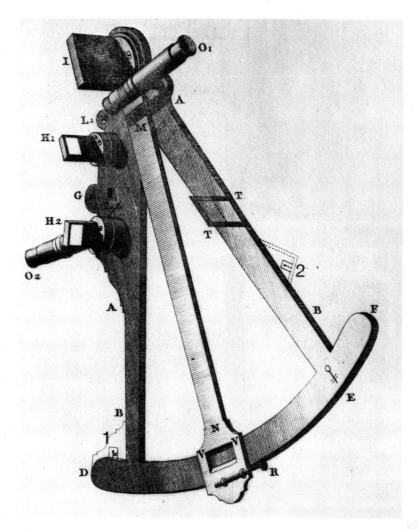

119. *The various components of the Hadley quadrant in its final form. Figure 5 shows how the mirror cd is fixed by means of the triangular plate (fig. 6) with three studs and the set screw S. There seems to be no provision for perpendicular adjustment as the square plate (fig. 2) cannot be inclined. The same applies to the small mirrors. On the other hand, the latter can be pivoted about their axis by means of the system shown in figure 11. Such adjustment, or collimation, was necessary to set the instrument at scale zero.*

The first well-made octants were equipped with the accessory shown in figure 23, which attached to a fitting on the back observation mirror. Before any observation of this kind was taken the main index arm was set to zero and the bar P, which is thus fixed to mirror H2, was placed in position 2. With this arrangement the horizon seen direct through T and the reflection of the horizon behind the observer should have coincided; if not, the angle of H2 had to be adjusted. The bar P was, of course, returned in position 1 for the observation itself.

118. *The illustration that accompanies the description of the 'English quadrant' in* Le Guide du navigateur *by Lévêque. Hadley's octant has taken on its final form, with the telescope on the usual side of the frame. The telescope 02 is used for back observations. The sight wire T is provided for sighting the horizon when taking this kind of observation.*

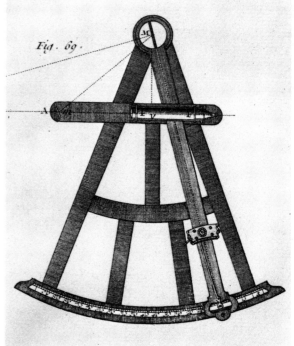

120. *Vernier octant perfected by the addition of a micrometer drum.*

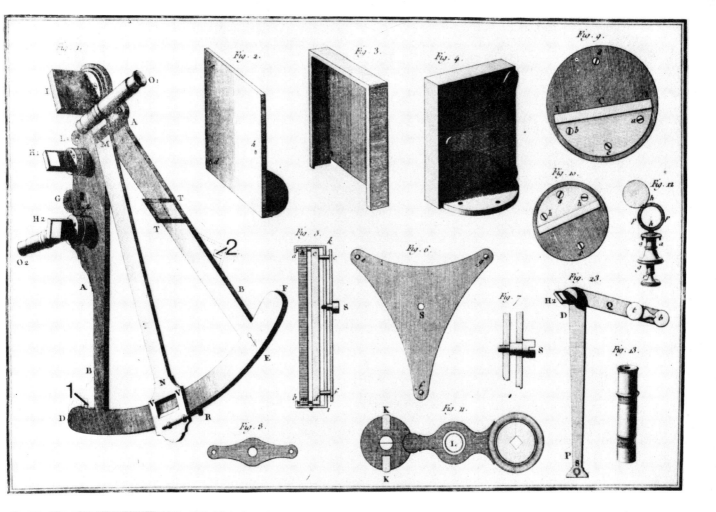

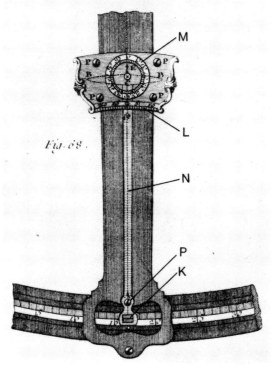

121. Detail of the vernier. Once the observation has been taken the index arm is locked; the measurement is then read first from the main divisions, in this case one-sixth of a degree, or 10'. The units of 10' are sub-divided by bringing the divisions on the vernier K into line with those on the limb by turning the knurled wheel M in the right direction. This drives a toothed arc at the end of the lever N, which pivots about point P. The number of minutes is then shown on the small scale L and the number of seconds on the dial M. One can well imagine the illusion of accuracy that this admittedly ingenious system created. There was little point in having precision to the fraction of a minute when one had to reckon with much larger errors in the division of the scale, prismaticity in the glasses and considerable eccentricity in the axis of the index mirror.

Front and back of two small octants, end of the 19th century. Instruments of this type were used by coasters and fishermen.

122. 'Eight bells of the forenoon watch!', engraving by Léon Paris. At the time of the noon sight on board a training ship there was no lack of hands to take the altitude. One seaman is noting the time on the deck watch in order to compare the rate of the chronometer. The officer of the watch from noon to four o'clock is coming up to relieve his predecessor, who is leaning impassively on the poop rail while awaiting the time to hand over. It was unthinkable to be a few minutes late at the change of watch. Everyone bends at the knee to the heel and roll of the ship under sail.

Finding the Position by Astronomic Means

Dead reckoning it was held sacred by routine-loving pilots, but it did have its limitations, as we have seen, and from the very early days of navigation attempts were made to use celestial navigation, which in fact merely provides a check on the estimated position, to solve the dual problem of latitude and longitude. As far as latitude was concerned, this had been achieved (precision apart) by the Portuguese navigators, who knew their latitude fairly well thanks to the astrolabe and the Alphonsine Tables, but how did they do it? We have to set aside our entire modern logic if we wish to understand how the seamen of that time thought and worked. Let us therefore revert to the methods used on Portuguese ships towards the end of the 15th century.

Upon leaving the Tagus the ships would await nightfall within sight of land on a known parallel of latitude, if necessary under sail; the pole star would then be observed with the astrolabe or with a Gunter quadrant for a given position of the Guards without bothering about the true position of the pole. Let us call the reading obtained $x°$. When a more southerly latitude had been reached another observation with the Guards in the same position would give a reading $x'°$. The difference between the two readings multiplied by 16.6 gave the number of leagues run along the meridian. This is obviously a far cry from today's neat and clear formula $L = N + D$, for which an appropriate correction is needed for the altitude and accurate tables for the declination. However surprising it may seem from the point of view of logic, this procedure devised by the Sagres school nevertheless produced good results.

Longitude remained the great problem. The uncompromising advocates of dead reckoning had attempted to impose a strange logic on the rectification of the estimated position as a way of finding the longitude by reasoning as follows: dead reckoning is admittedly inaccurate owing to errors in judging the real course and speed, but one of its two components,

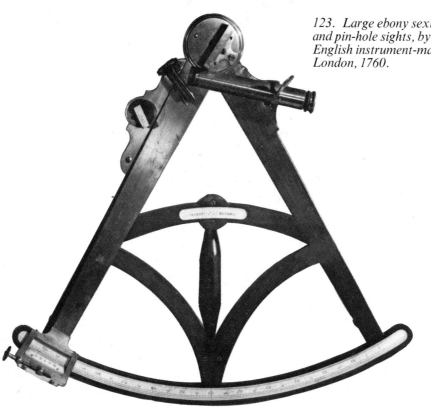

123. Large ebony sextant with telescope and pin-hole sights, by the celebrated English instrument-maker Nairne. London, 1760.

124. Title page of the famous treatise on navigation by Nathaniel Bowditch.

125. *Ebony octant for direct and back observations, beginning of the 19th century, by Arbon and Krap, Rotterdam.*

latitude, can be corrected by direct observation of meridian altitudes. Hence, if the error in latitude is the percentage $\pm$ p, the error in longitude can be corrected by applying this amount with the same sign. It was a tempting procedure, but totally without foundation.

Let us therefore look back at the other methods put forward for calculating longitude. As in principle a star describes an apparent movement of 360° around the Earth, it had long been established that when the star crossed the meridian all that needed to be known was the time (local time of the observation) at which it had passed over the prime meridian in order to determine how many hours and minutes (in apparent, mean or sidereal time) and thus how many degrees and minutes of arc one was from this point of reference. That was where the problem lay – in communications and time-keeping. A number of means of telling the time were soon devised, such as the conjunction of the sun and moon, lunar eclipses or the conjunction of the moon and the planets. As it was known precisely when these phenomena would occur at the prime meridian, all that had to be done was to note the local time when they appeared and work out the time difference in order to obtain the longitude. Eclipses and distances between the sun and the moon figure prominently in the *Almanacs* produced from the end of the 15th century onwards, such as the *Ephemerides* by Regiomontanus.

In 1610 Galileo discovered the first four satellites of Jupiter and noted that they were eclipsed. In 1664 Cassini drew up an eclipse table. In order to observe them one needed a high magnification telescope 15 feet long.

Without good instruments for observing the phenomena or accurate calculations of the time this method produced few results until the well

126. *Sextant by Bird, London, about 1770. Note the system of metal cross-braces to hold the frame rigid.*

equipped geographic expeditions were undertaken in the 18th century. Hence the advocates of research into good timekeepers continued to pursue their cause. In Father Fournier's work it is interesting to read the 17th-century view of the methods used until then for finding longitude.

That left the moon; in a later section we shall see how lunar distances were used, which had the advantage of not requiring a chronometer. Further details in this connection can be found in the *Abrégé de navigation* by Lalande, 1793, which describes the methods employed.

The Englishman George Graham (1673–1751) constructed a machine for determining latitude and the hour angle (and hence longitude) by introducing the data from two observations of altitude taken at a known interval of time apart. This was an attempt to solve the famous problem posed by John Douwes, the Dutch navigator, teacher of hydrography and naval examiner in Amsterdam in around 1740. The problem is nothing less than solving a system of two equations comprising two unknown quantities:

$$\sin H = \sin L \sin D + \cos L \cos D \cos P$$
$$\sin H' = \sin L \sin D + \cos L \cos D \cos (P + i)$$

where H, H′, D and i (a short interval in hours) are known.

In the 18th century, before the coming of chronometers, the hour angle was first calculated, using the estimated latitude, by means of the basic formula

$$\sin H = \sin L \sin D + \cos L \cos D \cos P$$

some three hours before the meridian passage of the sun, in other words when conditions were favourable, and then it was recalculated close to the time of transit. The value obtained for P was then used to find L. The calculations for P and L were therefore completely separate.

When chronometers began to be used on board ship Borda's formula for calculating the time from the altitude came to be used exclusively, the meridian altitude giving L at noon. No doubt the classic method would have continued to be used for several decades had it not been for the fundamental discovery made by the master of an American merchant ship (see page 111). Indeed, by 1828 the problem of longitude seemed to have been resolved so completely that the Board of Longitude, which had been set up in 1714, was dissolved.

127. All-metal sextant by Lenoir. Triple pin-hole sight.

128. *The very interesting position-finding machine by Edward J. Willis signed 'The Willis navigating machine. Marine type. U.S. Pat. Pending 1882. Richmond V.A. U.S.A.'.*

If the three components of the position P, L and D are set on three scales by means of the vernier cursors equipped with reading microscopes, the other two components (the estimated altitude and the azimuth of the star observed) are obtained 'without forcing' the precision mechanism. In view of its weight, the machine had to have integral carrying and fixing brackets, as can be seen in the photograph.

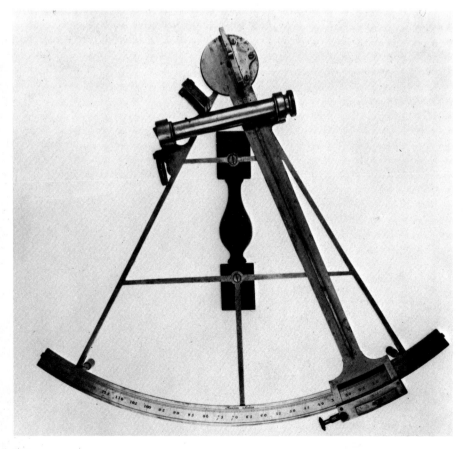

129. *Large sextant by the English instrument maker Ramsden. Note the telescope in the rest position. For taking an observation, the telescope was slid out and pivoted into the axis of the small mirror.*

Approaching the coast of Ireland on passage from the United States in 1837 Captain Sumner was very doubtful about his dead-reckoning position after several days of sailing in fog. However, a momentary break in the clouds allowed him to take a good sight of the sun. Sure of his altitude observation but equally certain that his latitude was wrong – the very element on which the entire calculation of position by Borda's formula rested – Sumner had the idea of calculating an average longitude by taking the estimated latitude that he had and two other values ten minutes of arc on either side of it. When he came to plot the three calculated positions on the chart he was amazed to find that they formed a straight line and he rightly concluded that he was on a position line. By a further coincidence, the line passed through the position of a lightship. He headed for it – a procedure that is nowadays called *homing* – and found it as expected. Sumner had in fact plotted the first *celestial position line* and had used it to avoid the dangers of the coast. He communicated his discovery to 'scientific maritime circles', whereupon it rapidly supplanted all the navigational methods used until then. Within ten years it had become institutionalised in France, where it was termed the 'Marcq Saint-Hilaire method'. From that time onwards navigation was based exclusively on the morning and meridian altitude position lines and on star 'shots' taken very close to dawn and dusk.

It was not long before refinements were introduced for the special cases of circumpolar and circumzenithal stars and for correspondent altitudes. It is fair to say that the celestial position line, which is universally understood and used nowadays, would be impossible without the sextant and the chronometer. The network of radio navigational aids is extending steadily across the seas, but on the best equipped ships three-quarters of the area of the oceans remains the domain of the sextant and the timekeeper, even though the former has been simplified, streamlined and 'styled' and the latter, now electronic, no longer ticks off the half seconds.

131. Double-frame sextant by Ramsden. It will be seen that the mirrors and telescope are completely protected by the metal bridge.

The final stage of the modern sextant before the advent of the drum micrometer sextant. This example, signed 'Heath & Co., London', dates from 1900. It has a toothed arc and an endless adjustment screw. The sighting arm is moved along the arc by disengaging the screw from the teeth by means of a pincer device. This sextant has a vast set of coloured shades and a Wollaston prism for dividing the reflected image of the star equally to simplify observations.

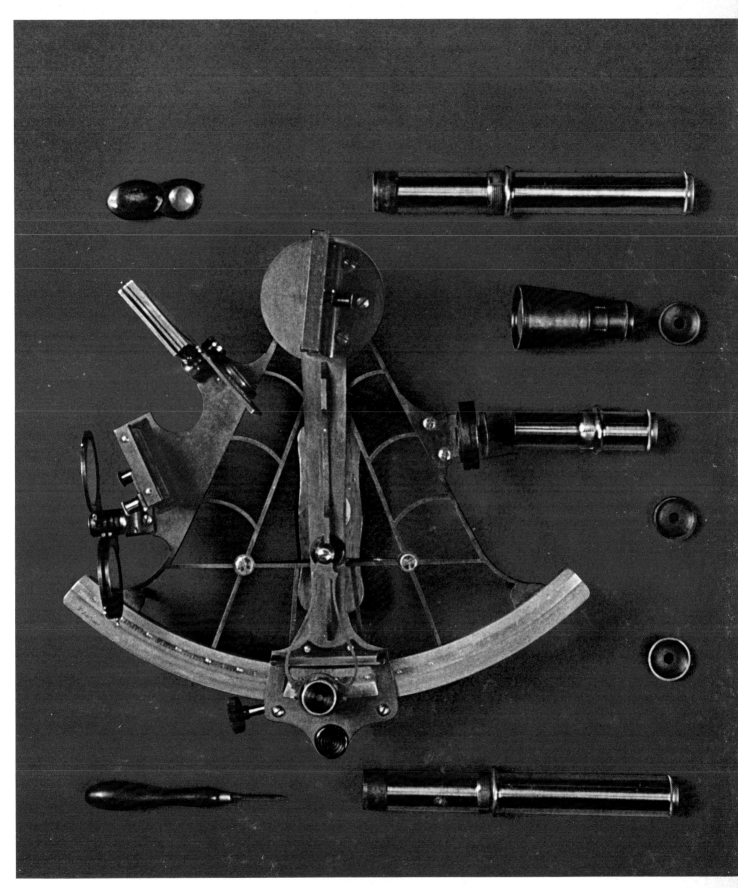

Observations Without a Horizon

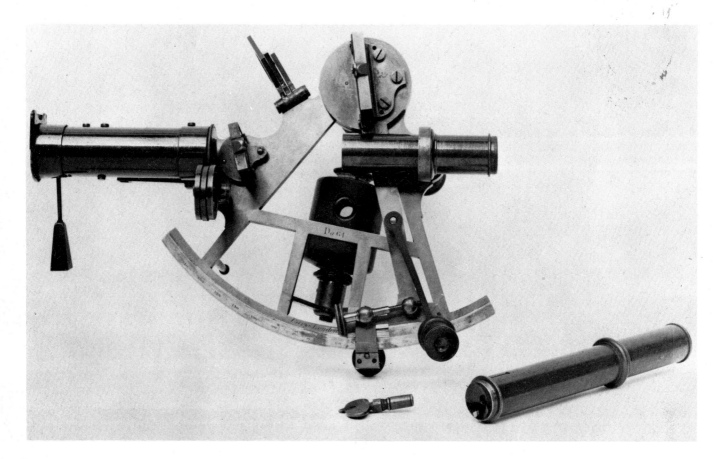

132. *a, b, c, d. How to take observations without a horizon.*

Before looking at the measuring instruments themselves, it would be well to recall the suggestion made in 1747 by Daniel Bernouilli, a professor of medicine in Basle: an improvised horizontal line could be established by rigging a lantern in a skiff at the 'exact' height of eye of the observer and placing it some distance from the ship (see small sketch in top right corner of illustration opposite). The altitude of the sun would not then need to be corrected for dip. This curiosity naturally remained in the realms of theory as there could be no question of putting out a boat topped by a lantern when an observation was to be taken.

a. – Father Pezenas, a Jesuit professor of hydrography and Director of the Marseilles Observatory from 1728 to 1749, describes a number of instruments for measuring the altitude of stars 'without seeing the horizon' in Mémoires *de mathématiques (1755). One of these is Elton's quadrant of 1730, which actually existed and was used at sea. It is a back-staff improved by the addition of two bubble levels, one for the verticality of the scale (2) and the other for the horizontality of the index arm (3); the other pieces marked are the horizon vane (1), the sighting vane (4), a pinnule and vernier (5) and a 'burning glass' (6), which can be placed in any of three positions on the upper arc depending on the altitude of the sun. The use of the instrument is easy to understand. The index arm is held horizontal with the aid of the level and the scale is slid through it until the spot of light falls on the horizon vane (1). No doubt there was a reflecting glass for observing the bubble in the level (3).*

b. – The principle of Radouay's sighting frame of about 1720, used in position b_1 for observing altitudes of less than 45° and b_2 for those of more than 45°. It has two pinnules (1) and a level (2).

c. – Like many other scientists, Hadley had the idea of attaching gimbals to the quadrant for use at sea. Nevertheless, there remained a residual movement that could be taken into account by means of a special level tube (3) containing a drop of mercury (4), which was arrested by closing a tap at the instant the observation was taken. The correction was shown on a small scale. 1: pin-hole sights and 2: the index arm. However, as the vertical was determined by gravity, it was the apparent vertical that was obtained.

d. – As early as 1744 Serson had the brilliant idea of using a gyroscope to steady a mirror for reflected observations. The instrument was subsequently improved by Smeaton. 1: the mirror, 2: the swivel joint supporting the instrument, 3: the gyroscopic fly-wheel attached to the mirror and 4: the ribbon for spinning the mirror. The instrument worked effectively for about a quarter of an hour. ▶

133. *Sextant by Cary of London with a Becher artificial horizon. It can be used with either a pinnule or a telescope. This type of artificial horizon depends on the verticality of a pendulum, which actuates a set of mirrors. It therefore indicates the apparent vertical.*

134. *The artificial horizon sextant by R. Rust is based on the very simple principle of a horizon marker held steady by a counterweight. In fact, valid observations could not be made on account of the unacceptably large errors due to parallax over such a short sighting distance.*

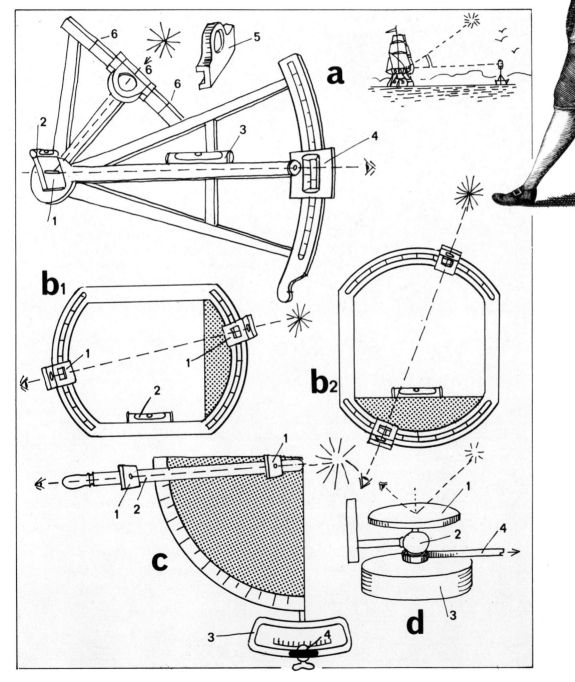

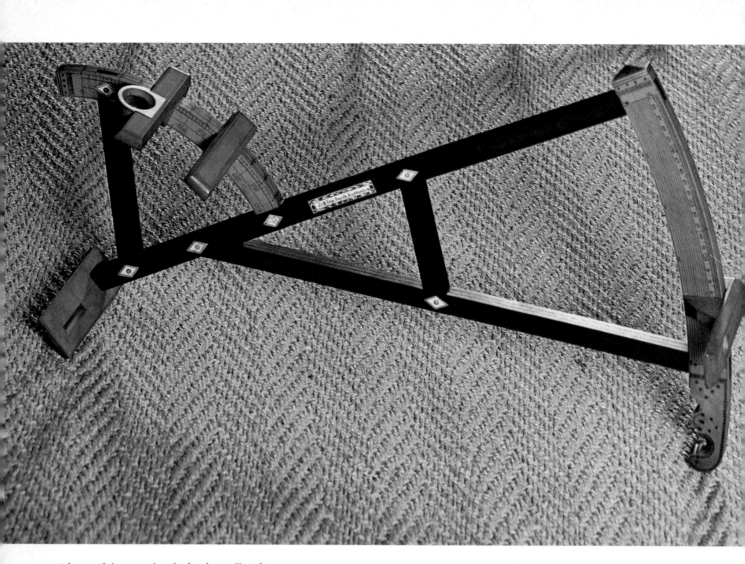

A beautiful example of a back-staff with insets, signed 'J. Kley fecit, Rotterdam', 18th century. The smaller arc has a lens as well as the traditional shadow vane; which one was used depended on the brightness of the sun.

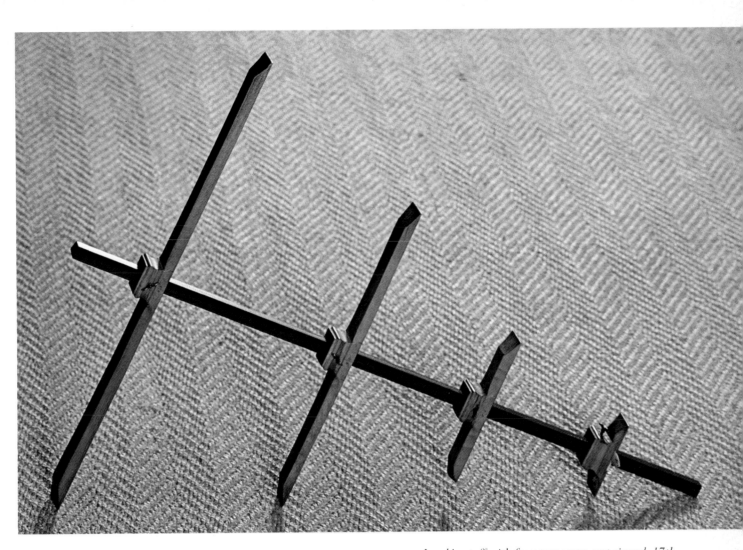

Jacob's staff with four transoms, not signed, 17th century. The appropriate transom was used depending on the altitude of the sun and the latitude. The measurement scales marked on the four sides of the square-section staff each correspond to one of the transoms.

135. *Sextant with gyroscopic horizon by Admiral Fleuriais. A gyroscope and a sighting system with a horizontal line to provide the artificial horizon are attached to a classical sextant, albeit of small dimensions, by Lorieux, Le Petit, Succr.*

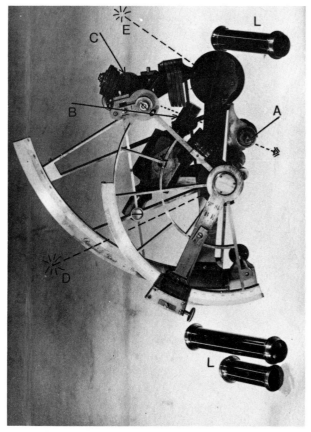

136. *Double sextant by Rowland, marked 'Rowland's Patent à Paris, 1834'. The collar for attaching the telescope (L) to the triangular positioning shaft A is missing. As can be seen, the smaller sextant is separated from its larger counterpart by the width of the mirror between them. The index mirror of the small sextant, which turns with the index arm, reflects the image of a point D onto mirror B and the index mirror of the large sextant reflects the image of a point E onto C. As B and C are in the optical axis of the telescope, the two images can be brought into line. The angular distance DE is the sum of the angles on the two limbs. This expensive, heavy and inconvenient device was probably the most complicated of the instruments designed for measuring wide angles and it was rarely seen at sea.*

118

Vermessungsquintant mit Trommelablesung.

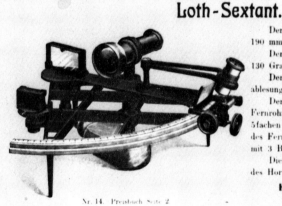

Nr. 13. Preisbuch Seite 2.

Der Radius ist bei dem Noniusschnitt 150 mm.

Der grösste zu messende Winkel beträgt 135 Grad.

Der Limbus ist in ganze Grade, die Trommel in ganze oder halbe Minuten geteilt, wie bei der **Bestellung** angegeben wird.

Der Quintant wird mit nur einem terrestrischen Fernrohr von 37 mm Objektivöffnung und einer 3 fachen Vergrösserung geliefert. Vor dem Okular des Fernrohres befindet sich eine Revolverblende mit 3 Blendgläsern. Die Schattengläser fehlen gänzlich.

Bestell-Bezeichnung: Vermessungsquintant mit Trommelablesung.

Telegramm-Wort: Trommelquintant.

Loth-Sextant.

Der Radius ist bei dem Noniusschnitt ca. 190 mm.

Der grösste zu messende Winkel beträgt 130 Grad.

Der Limbus ist in 30 Minuten mit einer Noniusablesung zu 60 Sekunden = 1 Minute, geteilt.

Der Sextant wird mit nur einem terrestrischen Fernrohr von 32 mm Objektivöffnung und einer 5 fachen Vergrösserung geliefert. Vor dem Okular des Fernrohres befindet sich eine Revolverblende mit 3 Blendgläsern.

Die Schattengläser, sowie der unbelegte Teil des Horizontspiegels fehlen vollständig.

Bestell-Bezeichnung: Loth-Sextant.

Telegramm-Wort: Loth.

Nr. 14. Preisbuch Seite 2

137. Facsimile of a page from the general catalogue published in about 1902 by the firm of Plath, showing two 'quintants' manufactured by this famous German company at the turn of the century. The extraordinary modernity of the upper instrument is apparent in its general design and the arrangement of the drum micrometer. The limb of the quintant, which was used for hydrography and for measuring lunar distances, was the fifth part of a full circle but could record angles twice as wide, in other words up to 144°, in accordance with the principle of double reflections. In fact the limb is graduated to just over 150°.

119

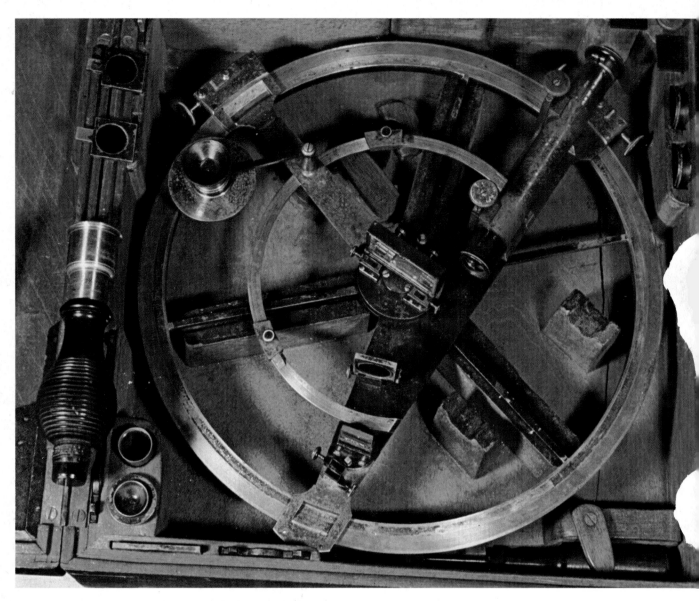

Reflecting circle by Jecker, Paris, end of the 18th century (see page 125).

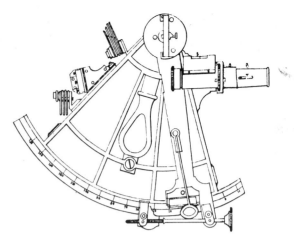

138. 'Fog horizon' by M. Davidson, 1880. The artificial horizon consists of a bubble level.

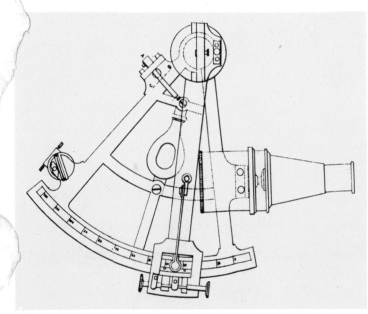

139. Elongating lens by M. Laurent, 1880. An interesting means of taking direct observations of the true centre of the sun.

140. Modern star globe, about 1920.

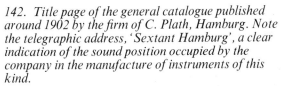

141. *Pocket sextant by Dollond in its case.*

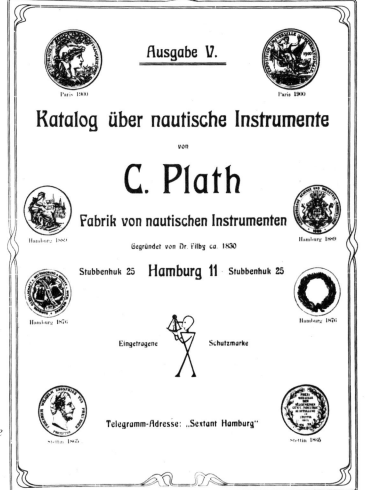

142. *Title page of the general catalogue published around 1902 by the firm of C. Plath, Hamburg. Note the telegraphic address, 'Sextant Hamburg', a clear indication of the sound position occupied by the company in the manufacture of instruments of this kind.*

The Art of Navigating by the Moon

143. *Woodcut from a 17th-century Portuguese calendar.*

The rapid movement of the moon across the celestial sphere and its predictable conjunctions with the fixed stars at set times very early gave astronomers the idea of using it as a standard timekeeper. Furthermore, the moon could be used in many ways – passage across the meridian, altitude, occultation of stars, 'appulses' (the moon and a star appearing simultaneously in the sights of a micrometer, heliometer or megameter), conjunctions of a star and the moon and distances between the moon and the sun. Of all these possibilities only observations of distances were adopted for use at sea.

The problem to be solved is as follows: 'Suppose that a star is on the orbit of the moon; the moon approaches the star or recedes from it by the distance it travels in longitude. 1. The distance between the moon and a zodiacal star is already known. 2. The distance between the moon and the star is calculated for the same time for the meridian on which the place of the observation lies. If these distances are identical, the observer is on the meridian for which the calculation was made; if not, the difference should be added to or subtracted from the calculated longitude, depending on the sign, in order to find the actual meridian of observation.'

We find this method being recommended in 1514 by Johannes Werner, in 1524 by Petrus Apianus, a professor of mathematics in Ingolstadt, in 1530 by Gemma Frisius, a doctor and mathematician in Antwerp, in 1560 by Pedro Nuñez and in 1600 by Kepler. Very precise tables were required. The Royal Observatory in Greenwich was founded in 1675 to study the movement of the stars and Flamsteed was appointed Astronomer Royal with instructions to apply himself 'With the utmost care and diligence to the rectifying of the tables of the heavens, and the places of the fixed stars, in order to find out the so much desired longitude at sea, for the perfection of the art of navigation'. Considerable work was carried out, but there remained an error of 5' in the tables owing to the lack of sufficient observations.

In 1714 the British Parliament went a step further and set up a Board of Commissioners for the Discovery of the Longitude at Sea and other matters beneficial to navigation.

In 1755 Professor Tobias Mayer of Göttingen submitted a set of lunar tables for which he received a reward from the Board of Longitude and in 1767 Maskelyne, the Astronomer Royal, brought the lunar distance method into general use. Longitude could be calculated to within one degree. At the same time he published the first nautical ephemeris intended for seamen.

In France Lalande published the method in the *Connaissance des temps* of

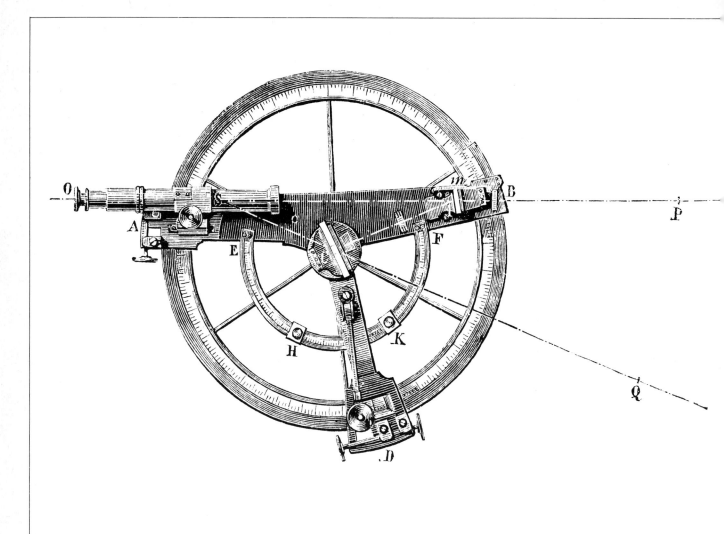

1774–75, devoting an introduction to it. Variations on Maskelyne's method of observation and calculation had already been used by Bouguer in 1753, Lemonnier in 1755, Pingré in 1758 and La Caille in 1759. The publication of Shepherd's tables in 1790 finally allowed precision to half a degree of longitude.

As was always the way when calculations became complicated, a plethora of graphic aids sprang up – reduction diagrams (Maingon), a spherical compass (Rochon), a calculating set-square (Richer) and a pair of four-armed dividers (Seguin).

The lunar distance method flourished. Suffren's fleet navigated by the moon (1780–1784) as no chronometers were carried, and in any case even at the end of the 18th century few people in the navy had faith in watches.

The modest initial observations made with Bouguer's heliometer and Charnière's megameter were followed by measurements of wide distances, which were unaffected by weather conditions (the motion of the ship) and independent of the horizon. This required measuring instruments with an angular capacity greater than that of the octant, the sextant and even the quintant. Hence the reflecting circle came to be invented, which could

The Reflecting Circle

144. The reflecting circle is used for measuring wide angles. It consists of a graduated circle mounted on a handle set at right angles to its plane. It has two arms, AB and CD, which pivot independently about the same axis. The arm AB bears a telescope, a clamping screw or tangent screw, a vernier at B and a small half-silvered mirror. The arm CD is fitted with an index mirror, a vernier at D, a clamping and tangent screw and a magnifier. Looking through the telescope one sees P and the reflected image of Q. PSQ is twice the angle between the two mirrors, in accordance with the principle of double reflection. The instrument serves equally well as a sextant, the limb being graduated in the same way to twice its true angle, hence from 0 to 720°. Its advantage, however, lies in the application of the principle of repeated measurements, which gives a whole multiple of the arc to be measured. Thus, if the observation is taken n times, the result is divided by n to arrive at the angle required and the error is automatically divided by the same amount.

The concentric arc FKHE, with its two slides H and K for easier repeated measurements, is called a finder arc or 'Mendoza concentric arc', although Mendoza's repeating circle did not have one, being fitted instead with a full circle concentric with the outer scale. If right and left observations are combined by turning the telescope alternately to the left-hand and right-hand objects, 'crossed' observations are obtained, thus obviating the need to determine the position of the arms in which the mirrors are parallel. This method eliminates errors due to lack of parallelity in the surfaces of the coloured shades.

Four adjustments have to be made to the reflecting circle:

1. to set the index mirror perpendicular to the plane of the limb;
2. to set the small mirror perpendicular to the plane of the limb;
3. to set the optical axis of the telescope parallel to the plane of the limb;
4. to adjust the cursors.

The residual instrument error is the angular distance between 0 on the limb and 0 on the vernier.

Further details on the use of the reflecting circle may be found in the Dictionnaire des mathématiques appliquées *by Sonnet or in the* Cours de navigation et d'hydrographie *by E.-P. Dubois.*

encompass half a circle. Another advantage of the reflecting circle was that it eliminated errors in reading off. The principle of repeating angles was first expounded in 1752 by Tobias Mayer, who was carrying out surveying work in Germany. In 1755 a reflecting circle was shown to the Board of Longitude and tested by the Astronomer Royal, Bradley, and by Capt. Campbell. The same instrument was illustrated in *Theoria Lunae*, published in London in 1767. Borda modified it in 1775, using a shorter telescope and a small mirror at the extremity of the arm so that both right and left observations could be taken. Setting out from a different principle, Mendoza fitted a vernier concentrically with the graduated ring of the Borda circle in 1801.

A large number of reflecting circles were constructed to these two principles by English and French instrument makers, and lunar distances were used intensively until the 1850s, when ships began to carry chronometers. In France the publication of tables of the lunar distances for eight major stars in the *Connaissance des temps* was discontinued in 1904. On account of its ability to measure wide horizontal angles, however, the reflecting circle later developed into the stadiometer, the ideal instrument for hydrographic surveying.

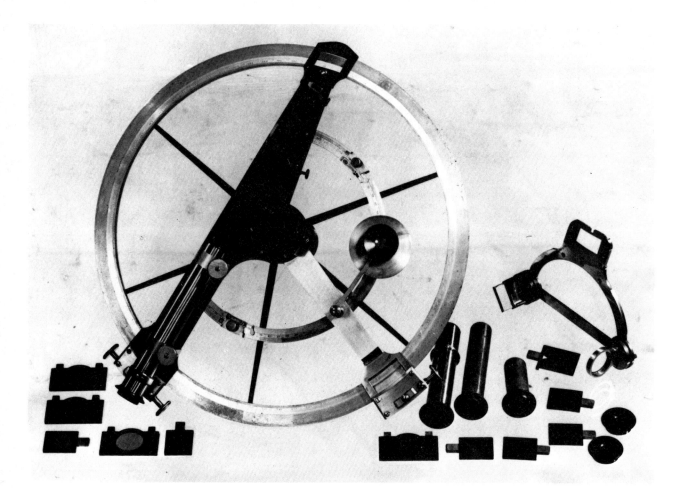

145. *Reflecting circle by Borda, used by the French navigator Dumont d'Urville (1790–1842). The instrument is shown with its principal accessories – coloured shades, eyepiece shades, telescopic sights and the bracket to hold the mirror and telescope for double observations.*

146. *Trade card of Lerebours, instrument maker in Paris.*

147. Mendoza reflecting circle. The two concentric circular scales and the characteristic stirrup supporting their hubs can be seen clearly. As it has two handles, the Mendoza circle can be used equally well for measuring both horizontal and vertical angles.

148. *Reflecting circle by William Heather, of the Mendoza double scale type.*

Terrestrial globe by Mercator, 16th century. Spheres symbolise the geographic knowledge of their age. From the 16th century onwards they were to be found in every library, and more particularly in every scientific collection. They ranged from extraordinary pieces, such as the pair of terrestrial and celestial globes 4.75 m in diameter made in 1683 by Father Vincenzo Coronelli, to more modest commercial globes of the kind produced from 1633 onwards by W. J. Blaeu, the official cartographer of the Netherlands. From that date onwards all globes had a horizon circle and a movable meridian circle so that the polar axis could be inclined to the appropriate latitude.

MODÈLE D'UN CALCUL DE LONGITUDE.

Le 20 Octobre 1776, étant par 20° 29' 29" de Latitude Nord, & par 67° 30' de Longitude estimée Occidentale ; (ce qui en temps donne 4 h. 30) à 2 h. 42' 20" sur la Montre, on a observé la Hauteur du bord inférieur du Soleil, de 39° 30' 18", ayant l'œil élevé de 18 pieds : après quoi, on a fait les Observations suivantes.

OBSERVATIONS.

	Temps à la Montre.	Diff. obs. des plus proches bords du Soleil & de la L.	Hauteurs observ. du bord inférieur du Soleil.	Haut. urs obser. du bord inf. de la Lune.
	4ʰ 2' 15"	94° 51' 25"	20° 26' 36"	32° 15' 30"
	4 17 16	95 3 18	17 19 6	34 55 30
	4 25 15	95 7 14	15 45 21	36 15 30
	4 30 15	95 7 51	14 41 53	37 10 30
Somme	17 14 56	380 15 48	68 12 36	140 37 0
Dont le quart. . .	4ʰ 18' 44"	95° 3' 57"	17° 3' 14"	35° 9' 15"
	Heur. moyenne.	Diff. moyenne.	Haut. moyenne.	Haut. moyenne.

CALCUL DE L'HEURE VRAIE, Comptée sur le Vaisseau.

CORRECTION DE LA HAUTEUR.

Hauteur observée du bord inférieur du Soleil . . . . 39° 30' 18"
Inclinaison de l'Horison, pour 18 pieds, Soustractive 4 21
Hauteur apparente du bord inférieur. 39 25 57
Réfraction Soustractive 1 20
. . . . 39 24 37
Parallaxe Additive 7
Hauteur vraie du bord inférieur 39 24 44
Demi-Diamètre Additif 16 8
Hauteur vraie du centre du Soleil 39 40 52
Distance vraie du Soleil au Zénith . . . . 50° 19' 8"

CALCUL DE LA DÉCLINAISON.

Différence Occidentale des Méridiens . . . . 4ʰ 30' 0"
Temps Astronomique compté à bord 2 42 20
Temps Astronomique compté au même instant à Paris . . 7 12 20
Déclinaison du Soleil le 20 à Midi . . . . 10° 39 16
Déclinaison du Soleil le 21 à Midi 11 0 37
Variation en 24 heures 21 21
Variation en 7 heures 12 minutes 20 secondes 6 24
Déclinaison du Soleil le 20 à 7 h. 12 min. 20 sec. . . . 10 45 41
Distance du Soleil au Pôle élevé . . . . 100° 45' 40"

CALCUL DE L'ANGLE HORAIRE.

Distance du Soleil au Zénith . . . . . . 50° 19' 8" Comp. ar. Sin. 0.007705
Dist. du Soleil au Pôle élevé . . . . . 100 45 40 Comp. ar. Sin. 0.028388
Somme 220 35 19
Demi-somme 110 17 39
Dif. de la ½ som. à la dif. de l'Af. au Pôle . 9 31 59 Logarit. Sin. 9.219104
Dif. de la ½ som. à la dif. du Pôle au Zén. 40 47 8 Logarit. Sin. 9.815268
Somme des 2 Logar. Sin. & des 2 Complém. Arithmétiques . 19.070203
½ Som. ou Log. Sin. de la moitié de l'Ang. Hor. de 3° 7' . 9.533121
Angle Horaire en degrés . . . . 6° 14"
Angle Horaire en temps, ou heure de l'observation . . . 2ʰ 40' 25"
Erreur de la Montre A 1 55
Heure de l'Observation de la distance 4 18 44
Heure vraie de cette Observation 4 16 49
Différence Occidentale des Méridiens 4 30 0
Heure comptée à Paris au même instant . . . . 8ʰ 46' 49"

Calcul du demi-Diamètre de la Lune.

Diam. hor. le 20 à midi . . 31' 42"
Diam. hor. le 21 à midi . . 32 8
Changement en 24 heur. . 26
Chang. en 9 h. 47 min. . . 11
Demi-Diamètre 15 5
Aug. du ½-Diam. p. 35° . . 3
Vrai demi-Diamètre . . 16° 8

Calcul de la Parallaxe Horisontale.

Paral. hor. le 20 à midi . 58' 2"
Par hor. le 21 à minuit . 58 23
Changement en 12 heur. . 21
Changement en 8 h. 47 m. . 17
Par. hor. le 20 à 8 h. 47 m. 58 20

Correction de la Hauteur observée du Soleil.

H. ob. du b. inf. du S. 17° 3' 14"
Inclinaison Soustract. . . 4 21
Haut. ap. du b. inf. 16° 58 53
Demi-Diam. addit. . . . 16 8
Haut. ap. du centre. . . 17 15 1
Parallaxe additive . . . 8
. . . . 17 15 9
Réfraction soustract. . . 3 20
Haut ur vraie . . . . 17° 11' 49"

Correction de la Hauteur observée de la Lune.

Haut. ob. du bord inf. 35° 9' 15"
Inclinaison Soustract. . . 4 21
Haut. ap. du bord inf. 35 4 54
Demi-Diamètre add. . . 16 8
Haut. ap. du centre. 35 20 5
Correct. additive. . . 46 14
Hauteur vraie. . . . 36° 7' 13"

Correction de la distance observée des plus proches bords du Soleil & de la Lune.

Dist. observ. des plus proches bords du Sol & de la Lune 95° 3' 57"
½-Diamètre du Sol. . . . 16 8
½-Diam. de la Lune . . . 16 5
Dist. ap. des centres. 95° 30' 10"

RÉDUCTION DE LA DISTANCE APPARENTE A LA DISTANCE VRAIE.

Méthode de M. le Chevalier DE BORDA.

Distance apparente de la Lune au Soleil . . . . 95° 36' 10"
Hauteur apparente de la Lune . . . . . 35 20 59 Comp. arith. du Cosinus. 0.088504
Hauteur apparente du Soleil . . . . . 17 15 1 Comp. arith. du Cosinus. 0.019988
Somme 4 12 10
Demi-Somme . . . . 74 6 5 Logarithme du Cosinus. 9.437649
Différence de la demi-Somme à la Distance apparente . 21 30 5 Logarithme du Cosinus. 9.968074
Hauteur vraie de la Lune . . . . 36 7 13 Logarithme du Cosinus. 9.907294
Hauteur vraie du Soleil . . . . 17 11 49 Logarithme du Cosinus. 9.980137
Somme des Hauteurs vraies. . . . . . . 53 19 2 Somme des six Logarith. 39.402246
Demi-Somme des Hauteurs vraies. . . . . 26 39 31 Demi-Somme. 19.701123
Soustrayez de cette demi-somme le Logarithme du Cosinus de la demi-Somme des Hauteurs vraies. 9.951189 Idem. 9.951189
Reste le Logarithme du Sinus de . . . . . 34° 12' 43" . . . . . . 9.749934 dont le Logarith. du Cosinus est 9.917487
. . . . 9.868576
La Somme de ces deux derniers Logarithmes est le Sinus de . . . . . 47° 39' 3"
dont le double est la Distance vraie ou corrigée . . . . 95° 18' 6"

CONCLUSION DE LA LONGITUDE.

Distance vraie ou corrigée . . . . . . 95° 18' 6" Différence de Distance 1° 20' 30". Son Logarithme proportionnel 3495
Distance de la Lune au Soleil, à 6 h. 9' 16". 93 57 36 Variat. de Dist. en 3 h. 1° 34' 35" Son Logarithme proportionnel 2705
Distance de la Lune au Soleil, à 9 h. 9' 16". 95 32 11 Différence des Logarithmes proportionnels qui répond à . 2ʰ 33' 12", qui ajouté à 6 h. 9' 16", donnent 8 h. 42' 28". 700
Temps vrai compté à Paris 8 41 28
Temps vrai compté sur le Vaisseau . . . 4 16 49
Différence Occidentale des Méridiens en temps . . . 4ʰ 25' 39", qui en degrés donnent 66° 24' 15" pour la Longitude Occidentale cherchée.

149. *Worked longitude calculation for an observed lunar distance (between the sun and the moon) using Borda's method, reproduced from* Le Guide du navigateur *by Lévêque, Nantes, 1779. It will be appreciated that the complexity of the operation fully warranted the invention of the graphic aid shown on the facing page.*

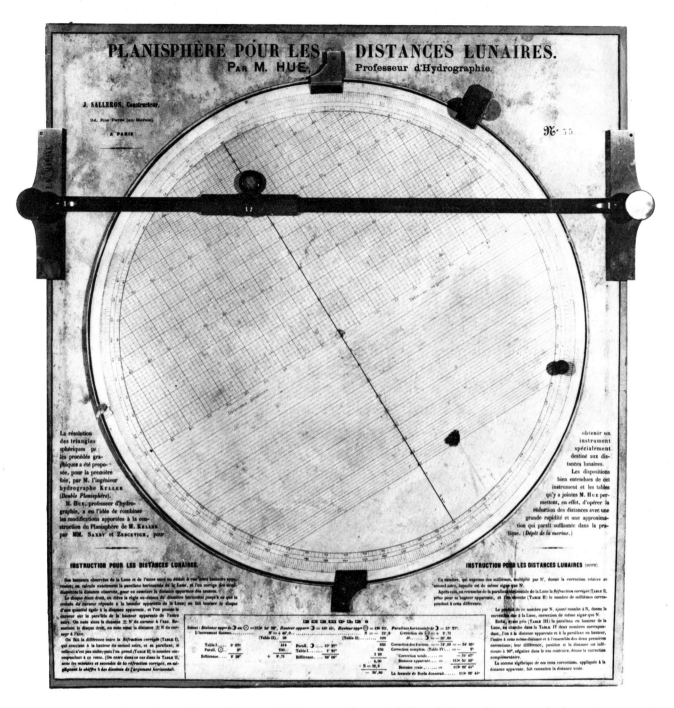

150. Seamen have always detested doing calculations with pencil and paper, preferring to use diagrammatic means. Indeed, our generation is acting true to form in adopting electronic pocket calculators. It was natural that a graphic instrument should come into being during the period when the lunar distance method was in constant use, between 1880 and 1910. The planisphere illustrated was devised by Hue, a professor of hydrography, and bought by the French Naval Ordnance.

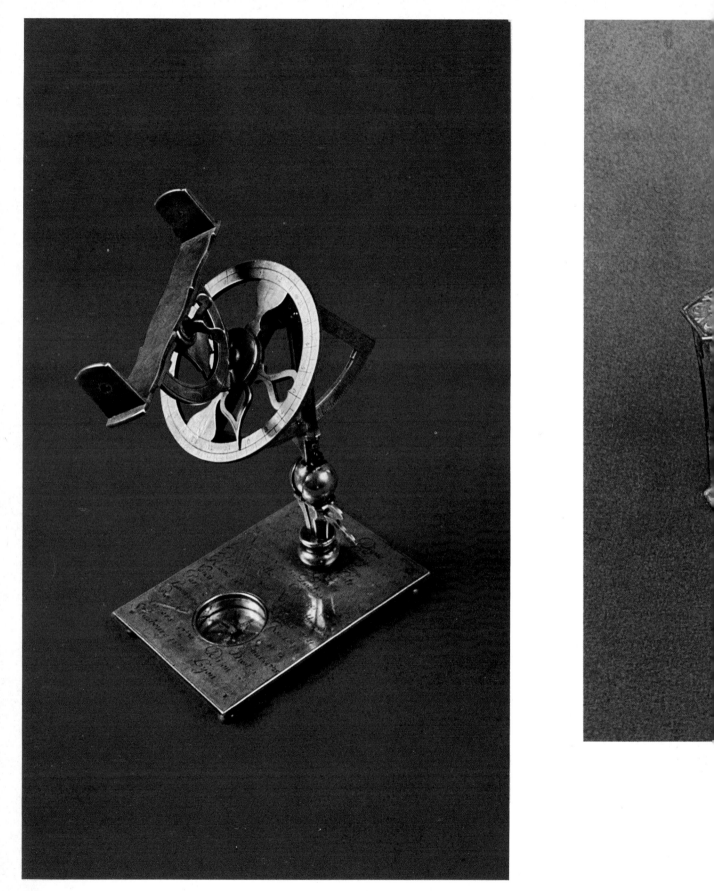

◀ Universal sundial with a sight rule. The equatorial circle is adjusted by means of the 90° sector, by which the altitude of the pole above the horizon may be set (by definition equal to the latitude). The instrument is orientated in the meridian plane by reference to the compass and the sun is sighted through the pinnules of the alidade, which moves the hour pointer across the dial.

Various 18th-century sand-glasses. Left: sand-glass set for measuring the half-hour and the quarter-hour. Right: classical two-bulb sand-glass. In the case of the three other hour and half-hour glasses with strangulated bulbs the quarters can be judged from the number of empty divisions.

133

4 · Time at sea

The element common to celestial position-finding, the calculation of speed for dead reckoning and even everyday life at sea is the time; hence ways of determining and keeping the time have been one of the major preoccupations of seamen since the very beginning of scientific navigation.

Before examining the means by which navigators overcame the problem of time, it may be useful to review the elementary concepts of the passage of time, which regulates the seasons, the months, the days and their subdivisions in accordance with the movement of the errant and fixed stars.

Time is one of the most basic concepts; if it is acknowledged that time passes and that two identical phenomena have the same duration, then one very quickly arrives at the notion of equal time spans and, consequently, the idea of measuring them. Chronometers, watches and clocks are instruments for measuring time by means of a series of identical movements, each of very short duration.

One of the earliest notions of a unit of time derives from the daily return of the sun. The solar day is the interval of time between two successive transits of the centre of the sun across the meridian of a particular place. This is solar or apparent time and the meridian passage marks solar noon. The solar day is slightly longer than the sidereal day. Taking the meridian transit of the sun as a point of reference, it will be seen one sidereal day later that while the Earth has described a complete revolution around its axis the sun has moved a certain distance along the ecliptic in the direction of its own movement, in other words in the opposite direction to the diurnal motion of the stars. Hence the sun takes slightly more than a sidereal day to return to the meridian, making the solar day about four minutes longer. Moreover, the duration of the solar day is not constant, since the speed of the sun's movement along the ecliptic varies, decelerating from the perigee to the apogee and accelerating from the apogee to the perigee so that the arc described by the sun along the ecliptic in a sidereal day is a variable quantity. Furthermore, on account of the obliquity of the ecliptic to the Equator equal arcs on the ecliptic are not equal when projected onto the Equator, with the result that the time required for arcs of the ecliptic to pass the meridian is not constant. The longest solar day occurs on 23rd December, which exceeds the mean day by thirty seconds; the shortest solar day is 16th September, which is twenty-one seconds longer than the sidereal day. It should be noted that we are not concerned here with the duration of night and day but with the interval between two meridian transits.

We must now define *sidereal* time, which is measured by the movement of the stars. The sidereal day is the interval that elapses between successive transits of a particular star at the meridian of the place of observation. In contrast to the solar day, the sidereal day is constant in length and slightly shorter than the former. Observatory clocks are set to sidereal time, a perfect unit of invariable duration, but for the needs of everyday life, particularly at sea and in the countryside where the sun is a constant companion, means had to be devised for converting apparent solar time (which can be observed from the actual position of the sun) into mean time shown by the clock, which marks off the units of time at a constant rate.

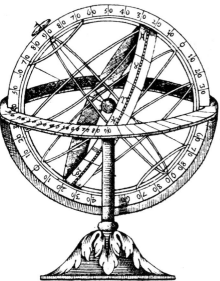

151. *Armillary sphere. 17th-century woodcut.*

Astronomers therefore dreamt up a *fictitious sun* which follows the same path around the ecliptic as the real sun and reaches its apogee and perigee at the same times. The second fictitious sun, which circles the Equator at a uniform rate and simultaneously crosses the same points as the projections of the first fictitious sun, is called the *mean sun*. Hence by definition the interval between transits of the mean sun at the meridian is constant.

Astronomers count mean time from noon to noon but the civil day begins at midnight. In order to compare mean and apparent time it is necessary to know the *equation of time*, which is added algebraically to apparent time. The nautical almanac gives the mean time at solar noon for every day of the year, in other words the number of minutes and seconds between solar noon and mean noon. As it is not convenient to have negative values, twelve hours have been added, time calculations being made at a remove of twelve hours. This value is called the equation of time.

Other elements of time that are of interest to the navigator are the lunar day and the lunar month. We know that some primitive peoples counted in terms of moons. However, the tidal cycle, which is linked directly with the phases of this planet, requires the seaman too to keep a check on the lunar calendar. The lunar day is the interval of time between successive transits of the moon at a particular meridian. Its average duration is 24 hours and 50.5 minutes in mean time. The synodic period lasts 29 days, 12 hours, 44 minutes and 2.9 seconds in mean time. During this space of time, however, the moon passes the meridian once fewer than the sun because of its own motion, so that the mean lunar hour measures 1 hour, 2.6 minutes and 2 seconds.

This brief recapitulation of some concepts of time will be a useful accompaniment to the examination of instruments based on the direct observation of the sun or moon, which are therefore graduated in apparent or lunar hours.

Let us return to the timekeepers that seamen have been able to use over the ages. Counting the number of days or moons certainly provides one elementary basis of measurement, as does apparent noon (the upper meridian transit) and apparent midnight (lower meridian transit), which can be observed only at the poles. However, the hours of the day had to be divided and marked more precisely.

No account of seafaring mentions a clepsydra or water-clock; the sandglass, on the other hand, was to be found aboard ship from the 14th century onwards, and although it was only used for measuring short intervals of time, it is easy to imagine that four-hour glasses might have been common at the beginning, as they were at a later date. No pendulum proved able to cope with the motion of the ship; sundials are depicted in this book and were actually carried by navigators in their baggage, but they could not be used on voyage as they were not fixed in the meridian plane and the plate on which the shadow of the gnomon fell was not steady. The only exception was the universal equinoctial ring dial, which was hung from a ring.

Pocket watches, which were produced from the 15th century onwards, were no worse at sea than on land, in other words they were pretty poor. It is fair to say that until chronometers were developed around 1760 the

Half-hour sand-glass or running glass, unsigned and undated, beginning of the 19th century. The bulb itself is 15 cm high and 8 cm in diameter.

Small fifteen-second glass, used for short measurements with the log ship. If a high degree of precision was not required half the ordinary measurement was sufficient; this also eased the laborious task of hauling in the log-line.

136

seaman's life was regulated by estimating the height of the sun, in the same way as the countryman, and doubtless by the turns of the sandglass, which measured the watches.

Right up until the end of the 19th century and into the 20th, life aboard ship was governed by solar time, that is to say the time of solar noon. The instant of culmination was the moment to strike eight bells, so that the hour was changed practically every day. This was of little importance aboard ships cut off from the rest of the world – indeed, it was better to live by apparent time. Calculations, on the other hand, were carried out in terms of the time shown in the chronometer, which was set to the time at the prime meridian (Greenwich or Paris). However, when the advent of radio communications required periods of radio silence and vigilance to be observed, the principle of *time zones* was proposed by the American Fleming and quickly adopted. France joined the system in 1911. Since then changes in time have been made in whole hours rather than by the equivalent of the day's progress in longitude. Clocks are put forward or back by one hour during the night, at a rate of twenty minutes per watch.

And now a brief word about the change in the date upon crossing the 180° meridian. When Magellan's companions returned to Europe in the *Victoria* after the death of the great navigator in the Moluccas, they discovered that they were an entire day out by the calendar. In circumnavigating the world they had crossed the 180° meridian without changing the date; it was the first time in the annals of travel and navigation that this easily explained phenomenon had been noticed. Let us take the case of a mariner heading west from Europe with a watch set to the time at his port of departure. For each 15° of longitude he covers his watch will have 'gained' an hour while the sun will cross the local meridian an hour later than at the port of departure. As there are twenty-four times 15° in circling 360° around the Earth, when he completes his circumnavigation and returns to his point of departure the navigator will have counted one day fewer than will have been counted on land since the beginning of his voyage. The error will be in the opposite direction for an eastbound ship, which will consequently be a day ahead on its return. Hence, without examining the problem in too great depth, the golden rule when crossing the 180° meridian is to add a day travelling westwards and subtract a day travelling eastwards. There is no mystery in this, as in fact the civil day begins with the transit of the sun at the lower meridian (180° meridian). Looking at the Earth from the north pole, the entire part to the west of the meridian round as far as the meridian at which the sun is then overhead is already in day $n+1$, whereas the remainder from meridian 180° to the sun's meridian is still in day n.

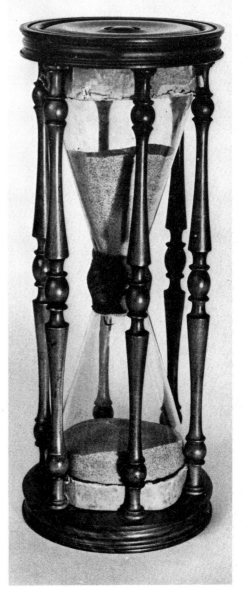

152. French hour-glass, about 1850.

Sand-glasses

153. Twelve sand-glasses of different types and periods. In the lower centre, detail of the three components before assembly, showing the two handblown bulbs and the insert with a calibrated hole that acts as a regulator.

Sand-glasses are simply clepsydras filled with sand. They are very early instruments for measuring the elapsed time and were to be found on board ship from the time of the first great maritime expeditions. The two conical phials are separated by a disc perforated with a calibrated hole and bound together with a network of threads. The very fine sand with which sand-glasses were filled was generally finely crushed eggshell or, according to the ancient chronicles, black powdered marble 'baked nine times'. On board ship the half-hour glass was turned on the dot of noon and then at each half hour until the next day. It soon became common to strike the watch bell whenever the glass was turned, which explains the old sailing-ship custom of giving a double stroke for the full hours and four double strokes at midnight, four o'clock, eight, midday and so on to signify the number of times the glass has been turned.

Accuracy was entirely relative, as will be seen from the account of the fleet of Duguay Trouin, which was caught in a thick fog off Spitzbergen in 1703: 'Fog is such a frequent occurrence in these parts that it led us into a most strange error. Aboard our ships half-hour sand-glasses are used that the helmsmen are required to turn eight times to measure each watch, which lasts four hours, at the end of which time the watch is relieved. It is fairly common, however, for the helmsmen to turn the glass before all the sand has run through in order to shorten their watch a little. This is called 'swallowing the sand'. This error, or rather misconduct, can be corrected only by taking the altitude of the sun; however, as we were without sight of the sun for nine consecutive days because of continuous fog and as in that season and latitude the sun only circles the horizon, making the days and nights equally bright, in the course of eight days the helmsmen managed, by dint of swallowing the sand, to turn day into night and night into day so that all the vessels of the squadron without exception found an error of at least ten or eleven hours when the sun reappeared. This had so upset the times of eating and sleeping that we all generally wanted to eat when it was time to sleep and sleep when it was time to eat. However, we did not take any notice of this until we discovered the truth by taking the altitude.'

Sand-glasses continued in use until the beginning of the 19th century. In France the large four-hour glasses were called 'battle glasses', as they were brought into use when it was feared that the blast from the ship's cannon would upset the timepieces.

We have already seen how the half-minute glass, or log-glass, was used with the log, but the sets of sand-glasses and very ornate timers are not at all out of place at sea, even though these beautiful examples of the goldsmith's craft are to be found alongside more prosaic sand-glasses equipped with beckets for hanging them from a beam hook.

Sundials

Sundials are as old as time, and it is natural that men accustomed to using them on land should have been tempted to take them to sea in an effort to determine the time, for want of any other means.

The diversity of sundials is practically limitless. It is customary, however, to divide them into two broad categories – *altitude dials* for regions where the sun is high (countries close to the Equator) and where the altitude, and hence the shadow cast, varies greatly from sunrise to noon, and *direction dials* for countries in higher latitudes where the sun's azimuth is more significant than the altitude. One can well imagine that for an observer at the Equator on the day of the equinox the azimuth will indicate nothing, as the sun will be due East from sunrise to its culmination and at noon will pass abruptly to the West, where it will stay until sunset.

We have limited the solar instruments shown in this book to those that are less sophisticated, better known or likely to have actually been used by seamen, leaving aside the magnificent polyhedral machines and multiple scaphes (hollow hemispherical sundials), which are more collectors' curiosities than universal timepieces that could be easily set and read.

The French word for dial, *cadran*, lends itself to confusion with *quadrant*. The prime purpose of Gunter's quadrant was not to tell the time but to show the seaman the altitude of the sun by using the pinnules and plumb line. Nevertheless, the sun sight itself and the vertical line for the day transferred onto a graduated curve also show the time. The sun's altitude is a function of the latitude, hence for a given altitude an equivalence table will give the time in terms of latitude and declination.

The nocturnal is a clock of solar time, although it is based on observation of the positions of the Great Bear and the Little Bear. The diptych dial can easily be adjusted for latitude by changing the point of attachment of the string gnomon, provided the latitude is within the range for which the dial was constructed. On the other hand the equinoctial ring with its style axis, which could be adjusted for any latitude, is an excellent travelling dial; the same system of adjustment is used in mechanical sundials with gear wheels and a sighting arm, which are incorrectly called solar chronometers, since they were designed in an age before the term 'chronometer' had been coined.

All these dials were certainly the solar clocks of seamen and travellers; they came fully into their own upon landing, when they could be laid flat and orientated correctly in the North-South axis.

A special place must be reserved for the universal ring sundial, which should have been called the universal armillary sphere, as it is in fact a miniature armillary sphere representing the celestial vault and has a stylised bridge gnomon in the form of a pinnule that may be adjusted for the season. Wright's universal ring dial was the true seaman's watch; it continued to be made until the 19th century and enjoyed great popularity until the very end.

Nor must we forget the ring dial resembling a napkin ring, which could be used perfectly well at sea with a little practice and was adjustable for latitude.

The broad principles underlying these solar clocks have been outlined here since the measurement of time in all its forms has always been closely linked with seafaring. As we all know, until fairly recently (the end of the 19th century) maritime expeditions still had the air of voyages of discovery, ventures that required pioneering equipment just as much as the means of peacefully mastering time and space.

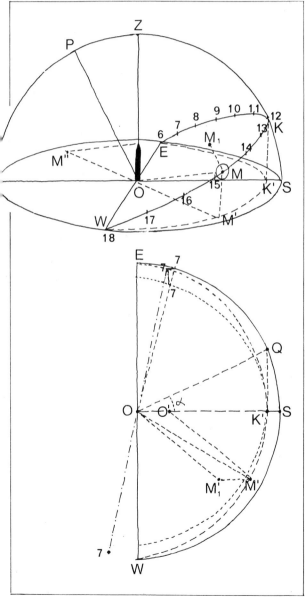

The Azimuth Dial

155.   The azimuth dial, which is an interesting instrument but impractical for reasons that we shall see later, is so named because of the successive shadows representing the azimuths of the sun cast by its vertical gnomon onto the horizontal plate. Dials of this kind are made for the latitude of a particular place and for the day of the equinox.

Let us visualise the celestial dome with zenith Z and the pole P. The large numbered semi-circle EKW is the path of the sun on the day of the equinox. It is divided into twelve equal parts representing the hours of the day. The point marked 12 represents noon and faces South. Let us consider the sun at 14.45, for example. The shadow of the gnomon will be parallel to OM, in other words OM''. If we wish to construct an azimuth dial a priori for a given latitude, we will note that all the projections of M are to be found on an ellipse with EW as its major axis and OK' as its semi-minor axis where
$OK' = OK \times cos\,(90° - Lat.) = OE \times cos\,(90° - Lat.)$. *Hence OQ is plotted with $x° = 90° - Lat.$ and the line QK' is dropped. Circles are then drawn with radii OS and OK' and divided into twelve parts. The point 7 on the azimuth dial will be at the intersection of the two parallels to OS and OE drawn through the points marked 7 on each of the circles. Since we are dealing with a shadow, this point should, of course, be transferred symmetrically in relation to 0.*

This graduation is valid only on the day of the equinox, when the sun's declination is 0° and the night is as long as the day. What happens at around 14.40 when the sun has reached an appreciable declination, for example when it is at M_1? At that time the sun will be in the plane running through M and P; using the same construction as before, the projection will be M'_1, so that the graduation for 14.40 inscribed on the dial will no longer apply at times other than the equinox unless the gnomon is moved from 0 to 0'. It can be demonstrated that $00' = R\,cos\,L \times tan\,D$. It is therefore simple to make provision for moving the gnomon in the direction of the minor axis of the ellipse. The height of the gnomon is determined at the moment of the summer solstice; its shadow should at least touch the ellipse.

The Analemmatic Dial

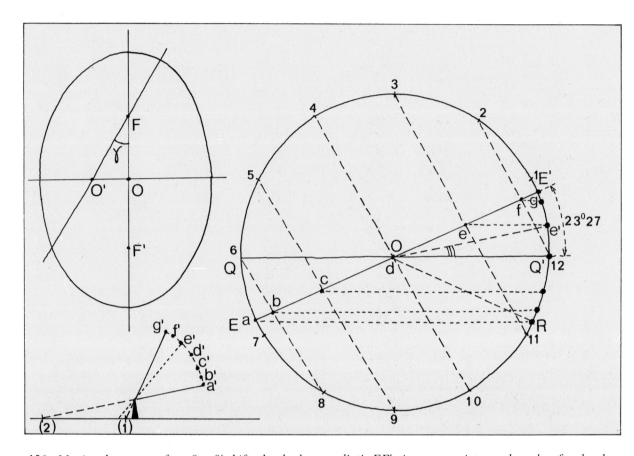

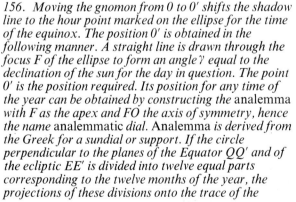

156. *Moving the gnomon from 0 to 0' shifts the shadow
line to the hour point marked on the ellipse for the time
of the equinox. The position 0' is obtained in the
following manner. A straight line is drawn through the
focus F of the ellipse to form an angle γ equal to the
declination of the sun for the day in question. The point
0' is the position required. Its position for any time of
the year can be obtained by constructing the* analemma
*with F as the apex and FO the axis of symmetry, hence
the name* analemmatic dial. Analemma *is derived from
the Greek for a sundial or support. If the circle
perpendicular to the planes of the Equator QQ' and of
the ecliptic EE' is divided into twelve equal parts
corresponding to the twelve months of the year, the
projections of these divisions onto the trace of the*
*ecliptic EE' give seven points – a, b, c, d, e, f and g ; by
projecting these points parallel to the Equator onto the
arc E'R we obtain the seven points of division of this
arc, which constitute the analemma, the construction
that by definition gives the altitude of the sun for the
twelve months of the year, the points of origin being the
equinoxes and solstices. Hence the angle Q'Oe'
represents the sun's altitude one month after the spring
equinox, or about 21st April. The seven points can be
used in this manner to determine the distance that a
given gnomon must be moved on a cursor for the dial to
read throughout the year ; alternatively, the gnomon
can be kept fixed and the scale shifted between the
extreme positions (1) and (2).*

The Diptych Dial

157. Diptych sundial in wood and paper, called a Nuremberg dial in spite of the fact that it has markings in English. In this system the style axis is replaced by a thread, the dial having been constructed for a particular latitude. It will be seen that the hour lines are marked on both the vertical and horizontal faces.

The Equinoctial Dial

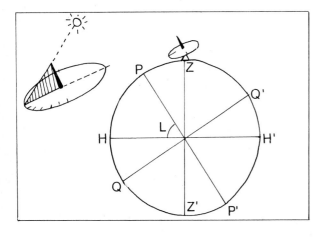

158. The equinoctial dial is very simple in concept; it has a gnomon parallel to the axis of the Earth and a base plate parallel to the Equator. The hour markings are spaced at intervals of 15° to match the hourly movement of the sun.

In this and the following diagrams, PP′ is the axis of the Earth, HH′ is the horizon, QQ′ is the Equator, and ZZ′ is the zenith at the place in question.

The Horizontal Plate Dial

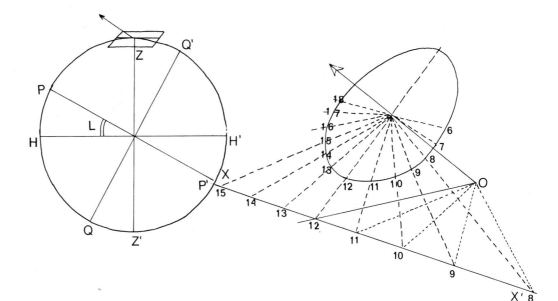

159. The horizontal plate dial owes its name to the fact that the base plate is parallel with the horizon, the gnomon being parallel to the axis of the Earth, as may be seen in the left-hand diagram. The procedure for plotting the hour lines, illustrated in the right-hand diagram, is as follows:

Suppose that a circular equinoctial dial is attached to the gnomon projecting from the horizontal plate of the dial at point 0. This can be divided into hours from 6 to 18, as is customary with these dials. Extend the plane of the circle to its imaginary intersection XX′ with the horizontal plate and extend the hour markings from the centre of the circle to the line XX′. It is then simply a matter of inscribing the horizontal plate with hour markings emanating from 0 to the points 8, 9, 10 etc.

The best examples of these dials are inscribed with zodiacal or declination lines, which are the traces described by the shadow of the tip of the gnomon at the different seasons of the year. These are usually hyperbolas or, better still, conical sections – that is to say parabolas when D = L, hyperbolas when D > L and ellipses when D < L.

160. *Butterfield dial with four positions for the gnomon from 40 to 60°, by Baradelle, Paris. The position of the gnomon is easy to adjust, the beak of the bird acting as the pointer. There are four horizontal hour graduations for 40°, 45°, 49° and 52°, the latitudes of the four main European capitals.*

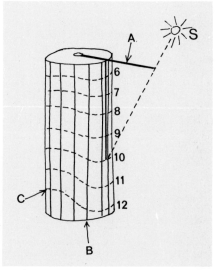

161. *The 'shepherd dial' or pillar dial consists of a cylinder and a gnomon A of fixed length. The generating lines B correspond to the months of the year. The hour lines C obviously depend on the changing declination of the sun. This solar clock measuring apparent time can clearly be used only in the latitude for which it was made. Correction tables can be drawn up for neighbouring latitudes and there are some examples of pillar dials with interchangeable gnomons and graduated sheets for different latitudes.*

The Vertical Dial

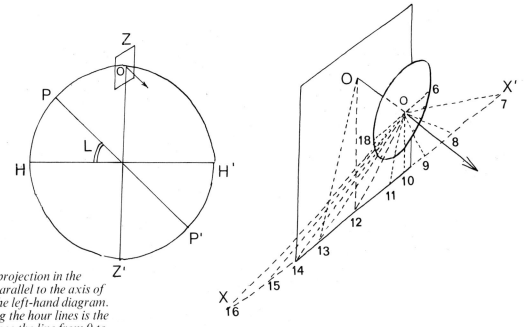

162. *The vertical dial has its projection in the vertical plane and a gnomon parallel to the axis of the Earth, as may be seen in the left-hand diagram. The procedure for constructing the hour lines is the same as before; for example, see the line from 0 to 13 on the plate of the dial. The fixed vertical plate does not have to be orientated in an East-West direction; if it is not, it is said to be 'declining' because of the declination of the plane of the projection.*

The Polar Dial

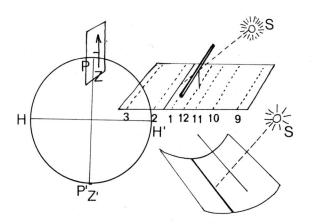

163. *At the pole both the gnomon and the plate of the vertical dial are parallel to the axis of the Earth PP'; hence the name of polar dial given to this type of instrument with a gnomon parallel to the plane of the hour lines. The shadows cast are therefore always parallel to one another. The interesting feature of these dials is that they can be used in any latitude. Sometimes the dial is made concave, with generating lines parallel to the gnomon, in order to keep the scale small. It is also possible to use a cone to create a more complicated instrument, such as those combining several systems found in cabinets of curiosities.*

164. *Mechanical equinoctial dial, made in Cracow, 18th century. The hour scale is inclined in accordance with the latitude and the horizontal base-plate aligned with the meridian. The thread gnomon is turned in the direction of the sun so that its shadow coincides exactly with a line engraved between the two supports of the thread. The needles of the large and small dials then indicate apparent solar time.*

165. *This ingenious instrument, made by De Kemel Bros., Antwerp, in about 1850, is mounted in gimbals so that its compass rose is, in principle, horizontal. It can show an azimuth direction by the large needle, a right ascension and a polar angle on the small dial (equatorial plane) and possibly a declination (close to the ecliptic). It may be a star-finder or a star globe but it also acts as an excellent sundial. In addition it can be used for calculating deviation and as a course corrector by taking predetermined azimuths of the sun. In the latter case it serves as a basis for adjustment of the compass.*

166. Trade card of the famous firm of Negus of New York.

167. Azimuth compass by G. Graydon, London, around 1890. The precision of the sighting system, consisting of a magnifier, pinnule and concave reflecting mirror, makes this an excellent sundial for telling the apparent time.

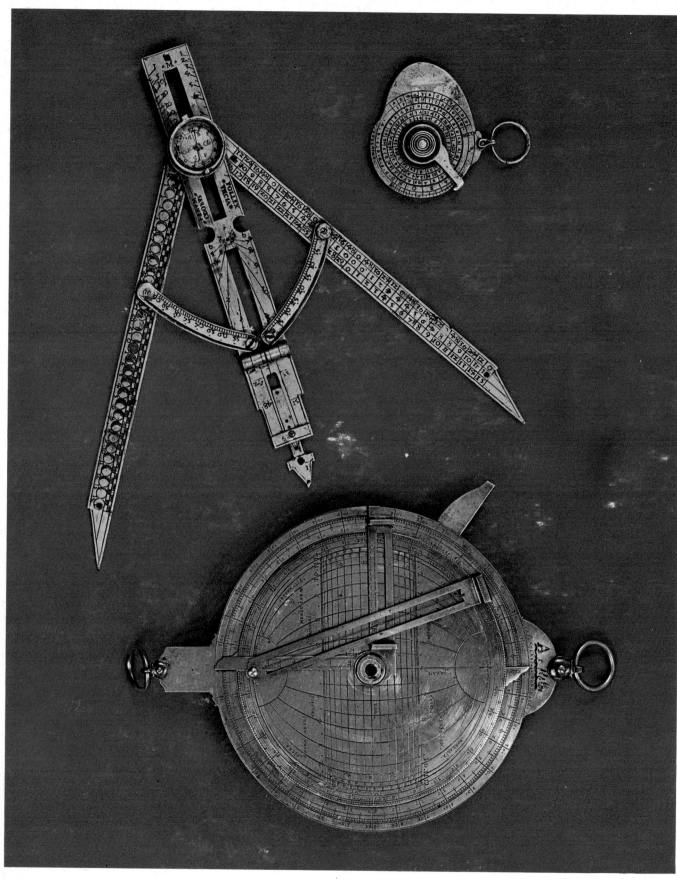

152

Upper right: *Tides calculator and lunar calendar by Sneewins, 1700. According to H. Daumas there were three Sneewins brothers, Anthoni in Delft, Henricus in Leyden and Johannes in Utrecht, who produced mathematical and astronomical instruments such as astrolabes, proportional compasses and pantographs.*

Upper left: *One of the multi-purpose instruments that were so common in the 17th and 18th centuries but whose mode of use has now been partly forgotten. It will be seen that it is principally a pair of dividers, the angle of which can be adjusted by moving the compass along the slot. When opened to 90° the two articulated curved limbs form a graduated sector. A hole is provided half way along the central bar for the gnomon of a horizontal plate sundial, the scale of which can be seen. The hinged lower section is also a gnomon which can be adjusted in height depending on the latitude. The left-hand limb is marked with the phases of the moon for each day of the lunar cycle. The right-hand limb carries a lunar calendar.*

Bottom: *Astrolabe with the Rojas orthographic projection, an instrument that was no doubt far too complicated for seamen and used only by astronomers. The back is a nocturnal, the sighting arm of which can be seen at the upper right.*

168. The reflecting circle by Richer, 1816, with three degrees of liberty (pivoting in the horizontal, vertical and lateral planes), was the observation instrument used for time calculations in terrestrial observatories during the first three decades of the 19th century.

169. *Equinoctial sundial of the Augsburg type by Negretti and Zambra, scientific instrument-makers in London, end of the 19th century.*

170. *Mechanical equinoctial dial by Franz Anton Knitl. The base-plate is set horizontal by means of the screw feet and plumb-line and the instrument aligned with the meridian by using the compass. The graduated plate is set parallel to the Equator depending on the latitude of the place and the movable arm bearing the pinnules adjusted to the month and day of the observation. All that remains to be done is to sight the sun to be able to read off the hours and minutes in solar time against the pointers.*

Sundials to Show Mean Time

171. Sundial for mean time by Oliver, London. This type of sundial would show solar or apparent time if it had a simple slit gnomon. However, this model has been adapted to show mean time by fitting a vane with a slot cut to a special shape based on the equation of time. The extreme upper and lower points mark the solstices (21st June and 23rd December). The narrow neck corresponds to the equinoxes (21st March and 21st September). The asymmetry of the shape is determined by the latitude of the place in which it is to be used; it could be symmetrical only at the Equator.

The Ring Dial

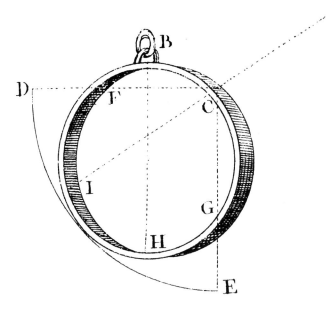

172. The construction of the ring dial, reproduced from the Encyclopédie of 1767. The pin hole, at point C, is positioned exactly half a quadrant above the horizontal.

173. Ring dial, Venice, 1564. The suspension ring is missing. The sighting pinnule is adjustable according to the season. The user must, of course, know the signs of the zodiac. The hour lines engraved on the inside of the ring are intersected by the seven month lines.

174. Consider a ring dial for a given latitude L. Let us suspend it by one of its radii in ZZ' and draw in the axis of the poles PP', the Equator QQ' and the tropics of Cancer (1) and Capricorn (2). The points M and N mark the greatest northerly and southerly declination of the sun. Light passes through a hole O drilled through the ring. Let us examine three specific cases:

(a) At the equinoxes the declination of the sun is nil. The furthest points reached by the beam of light at sunrise and culmination are shown by OA and OB. The beam therefore describes the arc AB;

(b) At the winter solstice the sun's declination is 23° 27'S, so that it is at position N; light passing through the hole O therefore travels over the arc AC (beams OA and OC);

(c) At the summer solstice the sun's declination is 23° 27'N, so that it is at position M and the furthest points reached by light passing through O are OA at sunrise and OD at the culmination, the arc described being AD.

It is therefore possible to graduate the inside of the ring with seven lines, giving six month bands, and simply to observe where on the band the sunlight falls to find the time (see lower diagram).

A represents the minimum altitude of the sun at sunrise, C the maximum altitude at the winter solstice (22nd December), B the maximum altitude at the equinoxes (23rd September and 21st March) and D the maximum altitude at the summer solstice (20th June). The concentric bands inscribed on the ring are date bands. The hour lines (the broken lines in the figure) indicate the apparent time at the spot on which the beam of light falls. Hence, if the date is approximately 12th March, the beam of light falling on point K shows that the time is either 10.30 or 13.30, solar time.

Some rings have two holes so that the inscriptions can be better spaced, thus improving legibility. In this case there are three bands on each side, one set for the months from September to March and the other for March to September.

These ring dials are calibrated for a particular latitude and are therefore useless elsewhere. However, in some examples the hole O is pierced in a cursor so that the graduation may also be used in a different latitude.

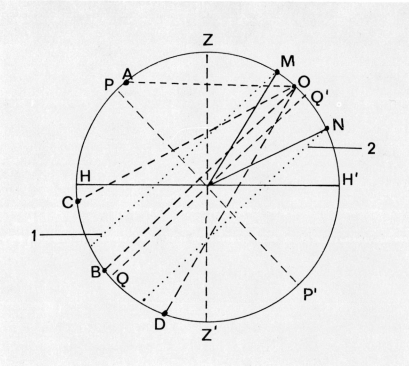

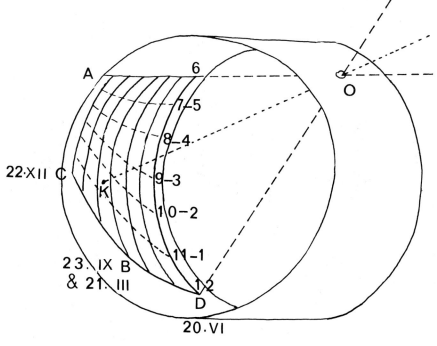

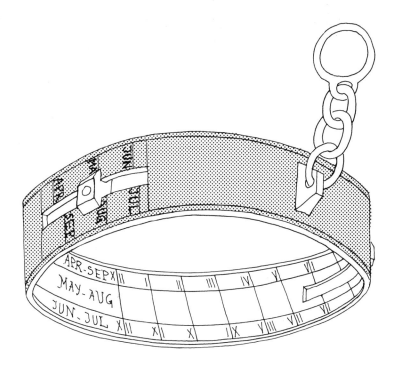

175. *Ring dial with two cursors. Signed 'L. Proctor, Sheffield', about 1750. Diameter 110 mm. The first of the hour lines, VI (sunrise), changes slightly according to the season. It is therefore necessary to adjust the position of the sighting hole by means of a cursor to ensure that the hour lines remain accurate. In fact, to make for clearer reading this well-made ring has six months on each side and two pinhole cursors.*

176. *Ring dial with double graduation. The pinnule is slid to one side or the other, depending on which scale is being used.*

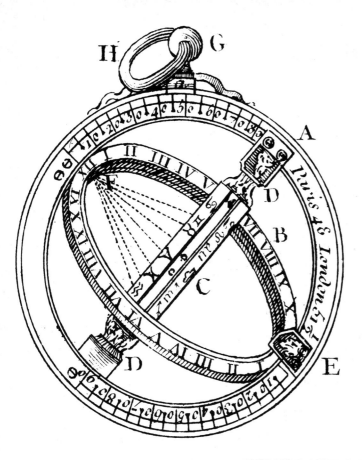

177. *The equinoctial ring dial, as illustrated in the* Encyclopédie *of 1767. The broken lines represent all the possible paths of light at noon depending on the month. The ring is set to a latitude of 48°, that of Paris. The engraving also gives the latitude of London – 51° 30'.*

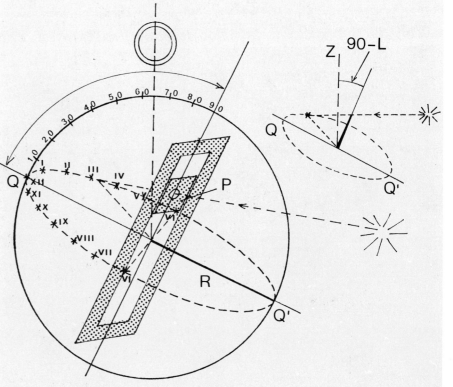

178. *Wright's universal ring dial is in fact a portable equinoctial dial. The small diagram, upper right, should help identify the basic components on the ring itself, the pinnule P being analogous with the tip of the gnomon. The instrument is used in the following way:*

1. Slide the suspension ring to the value of the colatitude $N = 90° - L$ in relation to the axis of the bridge.

2. Set the pinnule P against the graduation for the month, which depends on the sun's declination. It can be demonstrated that the distance from the pinnule (the figurative tip of the gnomon) to the centre of the instrument is $d = R \times \tan D$, where R is the radius of the ring.

3. Orientate the instrument in the meridian plane.

4. Read the hour from the shadow – or spot of light – cast on the ring, in this case 3.20 p.m.

160

179. *Three-part astronomical ring by Baradelle. The meridian and equinoctial rings are placed perpendicular to one another in the conventional manner. However, the central ring has two adjustable pinhole alidades. When the sun is sighted through the pinnules the point of intersection of the central ring with the equinoctial ring, which is marked in hours, indicates the apparent or solar time at the place in question.*

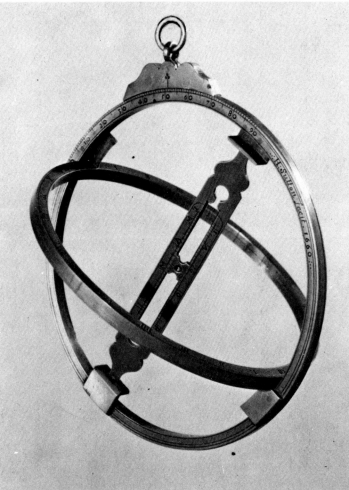

181. *Three-part universal astronomical ring.*

The traditional ring with pinnules cannot show the time at noon because of the thickness of the vertical meridian ring, which masks the light of the sun. The same is true around the equinox, when the pinnule is hidden from the sun by the equinoctial ring since sun and ring are in the same plane, declination being nil. This defect is offset by the double pinnule of the three-ring instrument. The hour has to be read between the two spots of light passing through the pinnules. With the astronomical ring suspended from Z, the hour circle is normally perpendicular to the polar axis; however, as the diagram shows, it has to be adjusted in this instance to take account of declination, in other words to form the angle α = (90° − L) − D with the line between the zenith and the nadir. If this is done, at noon the two spots of light will perfectly frame the graduation XII.

*182. Universal ring dial by Smith,
London, 18th century. When folded the
ring is flat. The stop fitted on the right-
hand side ensures that the equinoctial
ring remains perpendicular. The
suspension ring slides freely round the
entire rim of the meridian ring.*

Wooden nocturnal of English manufacture, about 1750. The front has the conventional circles and arm. This example could be used with both Bears.

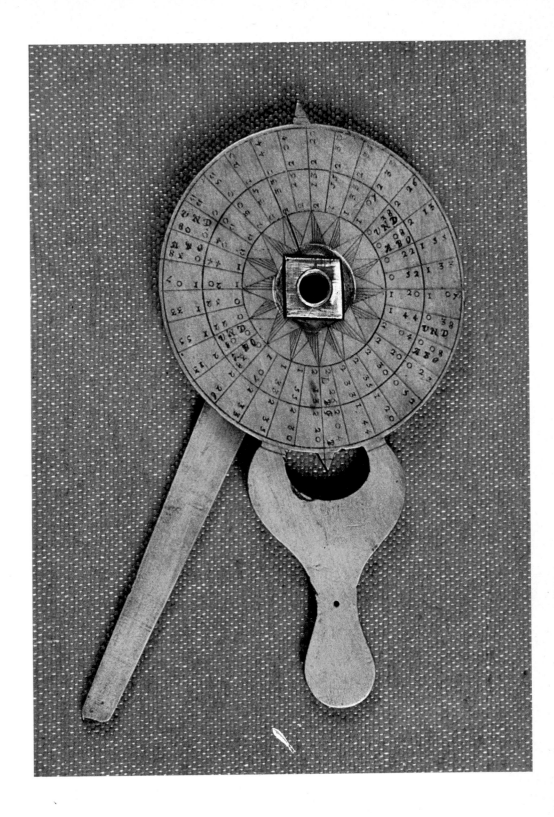

The back has a table of the polar angles of the Little Bear and of α and β in the Great Bear in terms of their alignment determined by the arm. ABO means above, or plus, and UND under, or minus. The highest figure shown on the scale, 2° 35', is the distance of the pole star from the pole in about 1750. By using this circular rule the altitude and azimuth at the pole can be found from the position of the pole star.

The Nocturnal

The nocturnal, otherwise called a star dial or nocturlabe by analogy with astrolabe, is as much an object of curiosity as it is a nautical instrument. It was used initially by astrologers, for whom the time is crucial, and later became widespread among dial makers. It shows local time at night from the observation of celestial alignments and although it is not very precise it was to be found aboard ships in the 17th century alongside sundials, of which it is to some extent the nocturnal counterpart.

The principle of the nocturnal is as follows: it is known that the line joining the rear two wheels of Charles's Wain (α and β in the Great Bear, the stars called the 'Guards') passes through α in the Little Bear, the pole star. This alignment describes a complete circle around the sky in twenty-four hours. Hence, if we know the angular position of this axis at the point of origin – generally midnight – we can ascertain the number of hours before or after midnight at which this axis occurs in another position by measuring the difference in angle. This is the principle underlying the simplest nocturnal.

The instrument comprises:

1. A disc divided into twelve parts representing the months of the year. Each month from January to December is indicated by its initial in anti-clockwise order. The point of origin, marked on the opposite side of the rim to the handle, represents the month and day on which the axis of the pole star and the Guards was vertical in the year in which the instrument was constructed, a detail that helps in dating nocturnals. The graduated scale is called the months circle and portrays the sky in equatorial co-ordinates for the year in question.

2. A second disc engraved with twenty-four divisions (twice twelve) in a clockwise direction pivots about a perforated axle fitted in the months circle. It represents the sky in the region of the pole and in use is superimposed on the celestial sphere itself. The point of origin of the graduations (12 o'clock), which is indicated by an index, is placed against the month and the day. For example, if the vertical axis representing midnight coincides with the alignment between the pole star and the Guards for the date of construction, one month earlier – 1st December – the point of origin must be moved by $30 \times 4 = 120$ minutes, or two hours, the sidereal day being four minutes shorter than the civil day. Hence the index is placed on the date, which makes allowance for this phenomenon of precession.

3. The third and last part of the nocturnal is the arm, one side of which coincides with a radius of the two circles described above. To use the instrument the time circle is first set to the correct date, the instrument is held up by the handle, the pole star is sighted through the central hole and the arm is turned so that it touches the axis of the Guards. The angle between midnight and the direction of the arm represents the number of hours before or after midnight that must be subtracted or added to obtain the true local time.

Some nocturnals exist, however, in which the time is read off directly from the central scale after the indices for L.B. (α in the Little Bear) or G.B. (α or β in the Great Bear) have been set, depending on which of these stars is observed in accordance with the date (month and day). It is then simply a matter of sighting the pole star and aligning the arm with the star being used in order to read the hour on the inner circle against the edge of the arm.

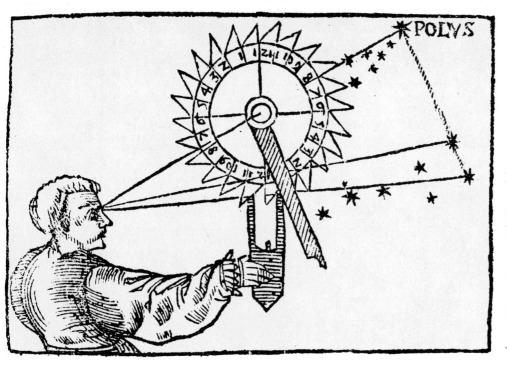

*183. Reproduced from
Cosmographia by Gemma Frisius.
The drawing of this very simple
nocturnal does not show the
months circle. The vertical position
of the midnight axis suggests that
the observation is being taken on
the day on which it is actually
vertical. However, midnight must
be at the bottom, so that the time
dial shows 1 hour 30 minutes true
local time after midnight, the
movement being reversed when
facing North.*

Another interesting nocturnal is that produced by Wright, which can be
used with the quadrant designed by the same inventor to take the altitude of
the pole star, in theory at least. Figure 184 shows how it was used. In
addition, a number of nocturnals doubled as tide calculators and others
were constructed to show the time from the moon. Nocturnals for the
southern hemisphere based on the Southern Cross are also believed to have
existed.

*184. This very sophisticated nocturnal by Wright
makes it possible to take the altitude of the pole star.
The relative positions of β in the Little Bear and the sun
are set on the date circle (6) in the centre of the
instrument by the difference in their right ascensions
(α). Once this angle has been set, the disc 4 is turned
by moving lever 3 until the arm (1) touches β in the
Little Bear. The time can then be read on the time circle
against the index 7, in this case 10.30.*

*The great novelty of this nocturnal, however, was
that it could be fitted to the end of Wright's sea
quadrant. The observer sighted the horizon and at the
same time kept α in the Little Bear at the edge of the
diameter parallel to the arm 1; the exact position of the
pole was then at point P seen through the hole 8.*

*This all presupposed veritable acrobatic skills to keep
the sights in conjunction, and it is hard to imagine that
this instrument was very popular on the poop deck.*

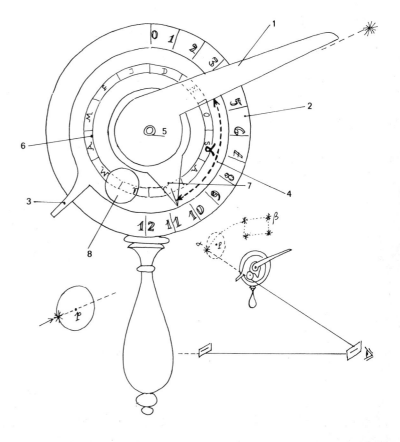

The Figure of the NOCTURNAL.

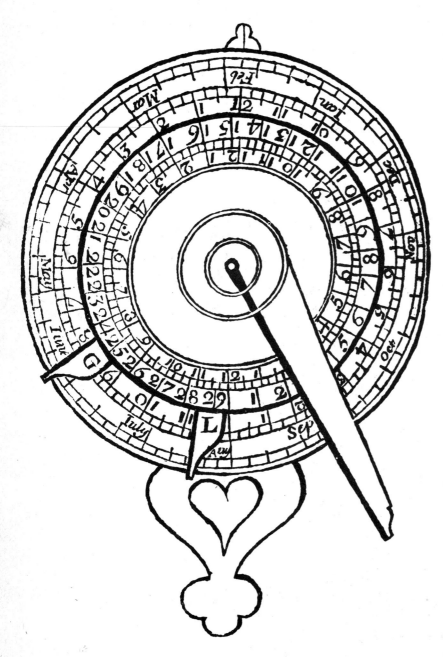

185. Drawing reproduced from The Mariner's compass rectified.

This highly perfected nocturnal consists first of an outer date scale. It will be noted that in the year for which the instrument was constructed the axis between the pole star and the Guards was vertical on 25th February. The time scale, which is within the preceding scale and marked with heavy lines, is used for adjusting the position of midnight as in ordinary nocturnals. The instrument shown in the figure is set for the day of its construction and the main arm, aligned with the position of the Guards, indicates that the time is six hours before midnight, in other words 6 p.m. in real local time.

Next comes the tide calculator. The establishment of a port is the number of hours that high water lapses behind the passage of the moon and the sun over the meridian (in other words midnight or zero hours) on a day of 'mean equinoctial syzygy'. At this moment the sun and moon are in conjunction and their declination is zero. By applying a simple rule of three the following calculation can be made: if high water occurs at 6 o'clock on the day when the moon is in syzygy at midnight (zero hours), then on the nth day of the age of the moon the time difference will be $\frac{24 \text{ hours}}{29.5 \text{ days}} \times n \text{ days} = x \text{ hours}$, in other words the amount by which the angular distance between the sun and moon widens each day before they are again in conjunction.

This calculation is easy to do with the tide calculator, which is simply a circular slide rule. The reference point 29.5 on the circle of lunar days is aligned with the value for the establishment of the tide, for example 6 hours. This increases with each day that passes. On the first day of the synodical month high water will lag behind by $\frac{4}{5}$ of an hour, so that it will occur at: $6 \text{ hr} + 1 \text{ hr} \times \frac{4}{5}$, hence at 6.48.

The establishment is 12 hours. It is the second day of the synodical month, so that there will be a corresponding delay of 1 hour 45 minutes. High water will therefore occur at 13.45.

It will be noticed that this nocturnal also has two index arms G and L. G stands for Great Bear (it may be either α or β) and L for Little Bear (or Kochab). The angle subtended by L and G at the centre of the instrument corresponds to the difference in the right ascensions of β in the Little Bear and α (or β) in the Great Bear. The time could be obtained by sighting the pole star through the central hole and aligning the arm with one or other of these stars. For example, for the Great Bear index arm G (or GB) would be set to the date – on the figure it indicates 25th June. Then the edge of the arm is brought into contact with the Guards or Pointers and the time is read off on the central scale, here about 6 o'clock. Using the nocturnal with the Little Bear the index arm L is set to the date, in this case 16th August, the main arm is turned until it touches β in the Little Bear and the time 1.40 is read off on the central disc.

186 (right). *Diagram of a nocturnal reproduced from the* Encyclopédie *of 1767. On this simple example the months circle around the rim is easily identified, with markings at ten-day intervals: 10, 20, 30; the initials of the months are engraved in Latin. The next circle gives the number of days in each month as a reminder. The time circle, which has a toothed edge, bears the index, set in this illustration to 16th April, the date of the observation. Once α in the Little Bear has been sighted through the central aperture, the arm is turned to align with the Guards (α and β in the Great Bear) and the time is read off on the time circle: 8.15. This is therefore local time, as it will be midnight when the line between the pole star and the Guards coincides with the 12 o'clock marking. As the observation is taken facing the North pole, the apparent movement is in fact in this direction, the stars rising in the East and setting in the West, so that the time is undoubtedly 8.15.*

187 (left). *Another simple nocturnal. In the year for which the instrument was constructed the vertical North-South line or meridian plane (the passage of β in the Great Bear across the upper meridian at midnight) occurred on about 12th May. The index of the time circle (the fleur-de-lys) is set to 2nd May, the date of the observation. Holding the instrument by the handle B, the observer sights the pole star through the hole G and brings the main index arm H into line with the Guards; the time scale shows about 6 hours 40, in other words 5 hours 20 after midnight. It is therefore 5.20 true local time.*

This system of graduation is less convenient than that of the preceding example. There is another fleur-de-lys index at the bottom, so that it might be 2nd November and 6 hours 40 minutes before midnight, in other words 5.20 p.m. local time. But is it dark enough at 5.20 p.m., even in November, to be able to observe the pole star and the Guards?

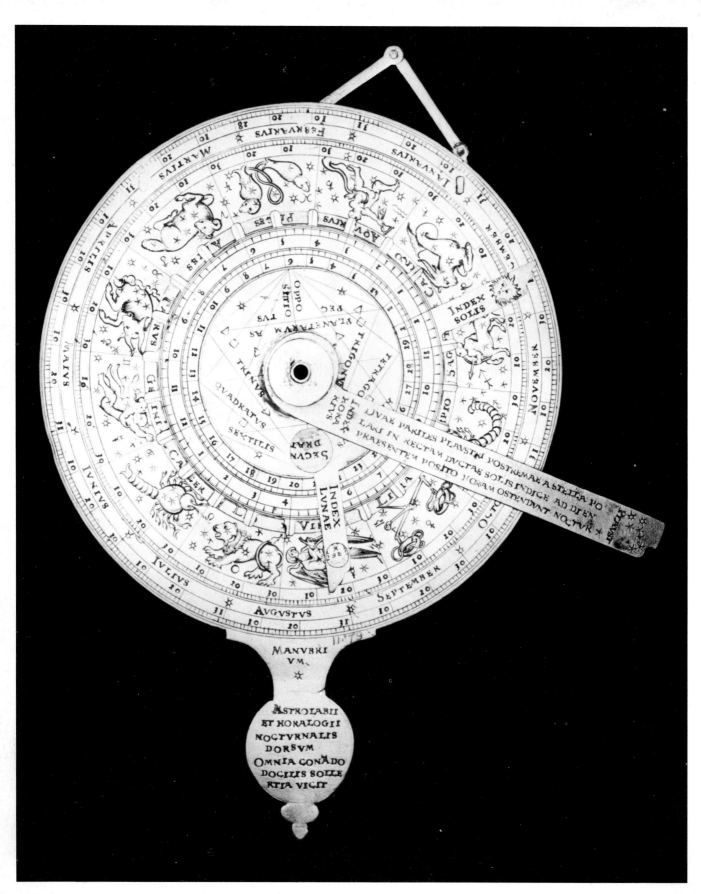

170

190. Iron 17th-century nocturnal, very richly embellished. This instrument has the two markers for the Great Bear and the Little Bear. The months are indicated by the signs of the zodiac on the outer date scale. It also has a lunar cycle for calculating the tides.

189. Nocturnal, about 1560, signed 'Amerigo Leona'. The face comprises a classical nocturnal. The back has two astrolabe pinnules for taking the altitudes of stars. A curious calculating system combined with the plumb line, the point of attachment of which can be seen, gives the time for the day in question at its intersection with the season line.

◄ 188. Nocturnal by Vogel, 1543. Classical arrangement of the time and date circles and of the main arm. It has a dial indicating the phases of the moon, equivalent to a tide calculator.

191. *Astronomical compendium, marked 'Rom
1582.'* Left: *a gnomon sundial for mornings and
evenings, graduated for the latitude of Italy.* Centre:
a nocturnal. Right: *another sundial.*

Marine Chronometers

The inaccuracy of dead reckoning became apparent as soon as navigators ventured far enough offshore. Countless methods for measuring longitudes direct were put forward, but they were all based on the same fundamental principle: 'The local time at a given instant being known, find the time at the prime meridian for the same instant. The difference gives the longitude.' Local time was known with reasonable accuracy, at least at midday, but that left the problem of the time at the prime meridian.

The earliest ideas involved grandiose systems created and maintained at great expense, such as a chain of ships anchored at various places in depths of no more than 300 fathoms (sic) that were to fire star shells at regular intervals to a height of 6,440 feet, thus giving the time at the prime meridian! It was a kind of aerial telegraph before its time and still utterly impracticable on the high seas, when one considers the difficulties encountered in

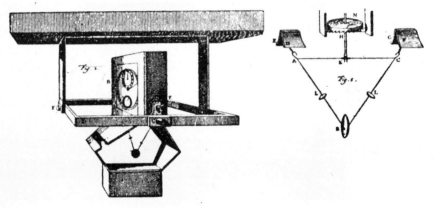

192. *Huygens' gimballed clock with a cycloidal pendulum, counterpoise and counterpoise frame arranged to accommodate the maximum amplitude of the pendulum. The escapement is of the verge type. The cycloidal checks are designed to keep the motion isochronous.*

193. *John Harrison's first clock, with wooden pinions.*

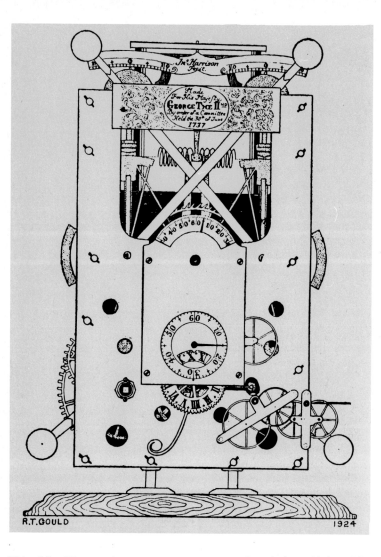

194. John Harrison's marine chronometer No. 2. Drawing by R. T. Gould.

maintaining light-ships even today. In any case, what system of synchronisation could have been used? Many systems of this kind were proposed but, as we have seen, navigators wasted no time waiting for them to be implemented, turning their attention instead towards observing eclipses of the moon, the sun and Jupiter's satellites and towards lunar distances. Some research was also carried out into magnetic deviation, but an eye was always kept on the supreme objective of developing a good time-keeper set to the time at the prime meridian, even though the incentives for discovery of a sure method of calculating longitude were not directed specifically towards clocks, as may be seen from the fact that the British Act of Parliament whereby the Board of Longitude was established in 1714 does not lay down the system to be used:

'The said Commissioners ... have full Power to Hear and Receive any Proposal or Proposals that shall be made to them for Discovering the said Longitude; And in case the said Commissioners ... shall be so far satisfied of the Probability of any such Discovery, as to think it proper to make Experiment thereof, they shall Certifie the same ... to the Commissioners of the Navy for the time being ... and upon producing such Certificate, the said Commissioners are hereby Authorized and Required to make out a Bill or Bills for any such Sum or Sums of Money, not exceeding Two thousand Pounds, as the said Commissioners for the Discovery of the said Longitude ... shall think necessary for making the Experiments ... The First Author or Authors, Discoverer or Discoverers of any such Method, ... shall be

Entitled to . . . a Reward, or Sum of Ten Thousand Pounds, if it Determines the said Longitude to One Degree of a great Circle, or Sixty Geographical Miles; to Fifteen thousand Pounds, if it Determines the same to Two Thirds of that Distance; and to Twenty thousand Pounds, if it Determines the same to One half of the same Distance; and that One Moiety or Half-part of such Reward or Sum shall be Due and Paid, when the said Commissioners, or the major part of them, do Agree that any such Method extends to the Security of Ships within Eighty Geographical Miles of the Shores, which are Places of the greatest Danger, and the other Moiety or Half-part, when a Ship by the Appointment of the said Commissioners . . . shall thereby actually Sail over the ocean, from Great Britain to any such Port in the West Indies, as those Commissioners . . . shall Choose or Nominate for the Experiment, without

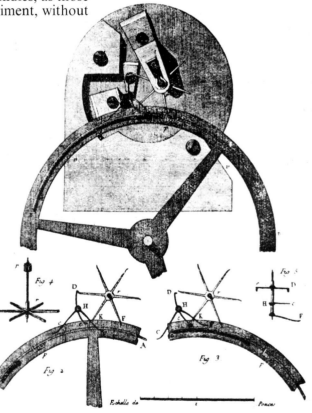

196. The detached escapement by Pierre Le Roy. Reproduced from the Mémoire sur la meilleure manière de mesurer le temps en mer, 1766. The balance has a short track on each side. The piece DHF shown in fig. 5 is the escapement of the six-armed star (fig. 4), which is connected to the wheel train and thus to the spring. In the detail at bottom left the star-shaped escape-wheel is held by D while the balance is rotating from left to right. In the right-hand diagram the balance is swinging back towards the left, D is released and one arm of the star catches on c, which is symmetrical with D.

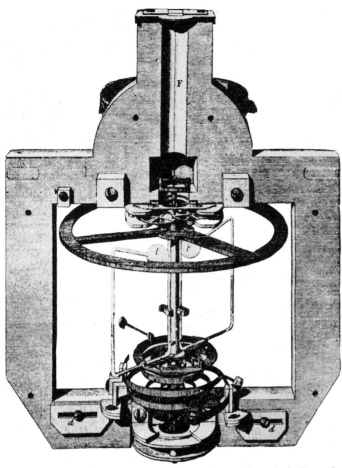

197. *The compensation mechanism of the longitude watch by Pierre Le Roy (engraving reproduced from Le Roy's* Mémoire sur la meilleure manière de mesurer le temps en mer, *published by J.-D. Cassini in his work entitled* Voyage fait par ordre du Roy, en 1768, pour éprouver les montres marines inventées par Leroy).

Changes in temperature are offset by two small thermometers set on opposite sides of the balance. These mercury thermometers, which are made of shaped glass tubes, contain alcohol in their upper portion. As the temperature rises the mass of mercury moves increasingly towards the balance staff, thus offsetting the retardation caused by the loss of elasticity of the two spiral hairsprings and also compensating for the outward movement of the mass of the balance owing to expansion. The resultant of the two moments of inertia, one centrifugal and the other centripetal, should therefore be nil.

This watch is now in the Conservatoire National des Arts et Métiers in Paris.

Losing their Longitude beyond the Limits before mentioned.'

Longitude was also being studied in most other seafaring countries. Philip III of Spain had offered a reward of 2,000 crowns in 1598 and in France 100,000 livres had been offered in 1600. In 1715 Rouillé de Meslay, a member of the French Parliament, bequeathed a sum of money to the French Academy of Science to provide for two prizes, one for research into the physical structure of the Earth and the other for the advancement of the science of navigation.

At that time the lunar distance method enjoyed the full support of astronomers, who were trying to refine it, for it still gave longitude to no better than one degree.

The efforts to perfect the chronometer had not received particular encouragement anywhere, and yet it was the time-keeper that would provide the most elegant final solution to the problem of longitude.

What was the technical standard of clocks in 1714, when the British Parliament passed the Longitude Act?

The first spring-driven watch, made by Peter Hele or Henlein, had seen the light of day in Nuremberg in 1500. This Nuremberg egg, as the watch was originally called because of its shape, had a verge escapement. It may be argued that Hele's 'egg' was scarcely surpassed by the spring-driven watches of 1700; they showed greater refinement in the finish of the parts, the attention paid to the reduction of friction and the more ornate decoration of the cases and balance-cocks, but they still had a considerable daily variation and, what was more serious, were very irregular. The verge excapement was also used in weight-driven pendulum clocks as it was practically the only effective system known, but these were much more accurate since they could be compensated for temperature changes and were protected from shocks by reason of their fixed position. The early attempts to produce a marine

English chronometer, end of the 19th century.

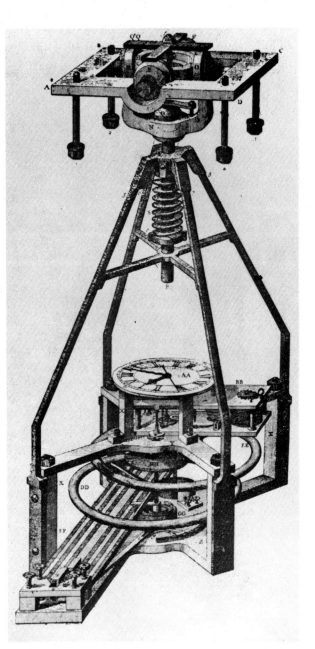

198. Marine clock No. 1 by Ferdinand Berthoud. Reproduced from Essai sur l'horlogerie, *1763. This clock is now in the Conservatoire National des Arts et Métiers in Paris.*

chronometer were therefore centred on the pendulum. In 1669 Huygens carried out the first tests on a marine clock with a cycloidal pendulum, which a Capt. Holmes found gave an error of 150 km in longitude at the end of a voyage to the Cape Verde Islands. Hence navigation by the clock was less satisfactory than by lunar distances. In France Dutertre was also working on a clock with two pendulums geared together, but the real solution was to be derived from another principle, developed by an obscure mechanic from Yorkshire, John Harrison, who was the son of a carpenter and had a mania about clocks. Through his true genius he swept away all the unresolved mechanical problems of his age and by making four clocks, each better than the last, achieved results acceptable for position finding at sea.

Born in 1693, John Harrison heard of the reward offered by the Board of Longitude and, having already acquired some experience in clock-making, set about building his first marine clock, on which he spent six years from the time of his meeting with the famous clockmaker Graham. The No. 1, which has two balances rotating in opposite directions and the grasshopper escapement that is nowadays so familiar to historians of clock-making, is compensated for temperature changes by means of a gridiron system acting on the tension of the balance springs. Completed in 1735, this sizable machine weighing 36 kg underwent sea trials aboard a naval vessel during a voyage to Lisbon. A brief mention appeared in the official minutes of the Board of Longitude: 'Mr. John Harrison produced a new invented machine, in the nature of clockwork, whereby he proposes to keep time at sea with more exactness than by any other instrument or method hitherto contrived.'

Harrison was awarded £500 as encouragement to produce a second clock that he already had in mind. No. 2 was completed in 1739, but it was essentially a further development of his No. 1 clock, with no notable changes. Without this time committing himself to a completion date, the clockmaker therefore set to work on a third time-keeper, which was to occupy him for seventeen arduous years.

In the No. 3 clock the opposed balances were replaced by circular balances connected together by wires as in clocks Nos. 1 and 2 but controlled by a large spiral spring common to both. The balances were compensated for temperature changes by a bimetallic curb, which adjusted the effective length of the hairspring and hence its period of oscillation. Numerous anti-friction devices were fitted and Harrison hoped to achieve precision of three or four seconds a week. However, for one reason or another the No. 3 was not tested at sea and work was immediately begun on a fourth.

This time it was a large carriage watch, 13 cm in diameter, without gimbals, so that it was simply placed on a cushion. The large balance had a diameter of 60 mm and the grasshopper escapement, which could not be made small enough, was replaced by a verge escapement, although a much improved one on account of the special shape of the teeth and pallets. Having failed to discover the detached escapement that separates the balance from the wheel train, Harrison invented a device that produced the same effect; this so-called 'remontoir' was a kind of intermediate store of mechanical energy. Completed in 1759, clock No. 4 was put aboard HMS *Deptford* in 1761. The five-month voyage via Madeira and Jamaica demonstrated the remarkable qualities of Harrison's clock, which varied by only 53 seconds in all, giving an error in longitude of 28'.

Would Harrison be granted the prize of £20,000 laid down by Act of Parliament? Sadly, many years were to pass before the great craftsman would receive his reward. Further trials were carried out on a copy of his No. 4 watch made by the clockmaker Kendall. Harrison himself was subjected to cross-examination by the commission of enquiry in front of the dismantled watch. Fraud? Mystery? Fluke? The Board found it hard to believe that it at last held the secret of a machine capable of solving the problem of the 'fixed point'. And yet there it was. However, ranged against it were the ingrained habits of dead reckoning and the opposition of partisans of the lunar distance method, which had cost so much effort, and who enjoyed the support of Maskelyne, the Astronomer Royal.

The Board of Longitude dragged its feet until a fifth watch had been built and tested successfully at Kew Observatory, thus clearly revealing the injustice done to Harrison. In 1772 the clockmaker was granted the balance of the reward after deduction of the various sums that had already been paid by way of encouragement. By then he was eighty years old and he died three years later. Shortly afterwards, however, the highly successful voyage of James Cook with Kendall's copy of No. 4 demonstrated Harrison's genius to the nautical and clock-making world and perpetuated his memory. Isolated, out of touch with the research of his time, John Harrison had produced a work of absolute originality, but it was so singular and so lacking in generally applicable principles that it died with him and the work of research was taken up again almost simultaneously by two clockmakers working in France, the Frenchman Pierre Le Roy (1717–1785) and the Swiss Ferdinand Berthoud (1727–1807).

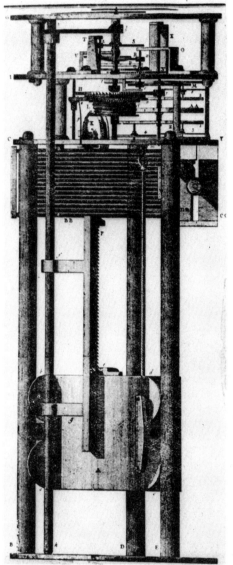

199. Weight-driven clock by Ferdinand Berthoud. In his various models Berthoud switched between springs and this system, which is heavier and requires guide wheels for the weight and a winding rack. Temperature compensation is by means of a gridiron.

McGregor chronometer seen from the side of the top plate as opposed to the pillar plate nearest to the dial. Above: the winding square (the axle of the fusee) surrounded by the winder collar intended as much to exclude dust as to guide the key. Centre: the balance wheel held in the balance cock or bridge, which supports the upper end of the staff. Right: the barrel click, for adjusting the tension of the main spring. Between the two plates can be seen the pillars or columns that maintain the correct distance between them.

In 1766 Pierre Le Roy presented a longitude clock to the French Academy of Science accompanied by a paper published four years later under the title *Mémoire sur la meilleure manière de mesurer le temps en mer*, in which all the main principles of modern chronometry are to be found. Power is provided by a spring, the large and heavy circular balance 108 mm in diameter is suspended by a steel wire and the staff is set in rollers. As the suspension wire would produce too long a period of oscillation, there are two large, flat, isochronous balance springs that reduce the beat to the half second. The isochronism of the hairspring, the first main principle of chronometry, had been discovered.

Furthermore, Le Roy had used a special kind of escapement which was none other than the *detached escapement* that had been sought for so long. Except during a small fraction of its movement, during which it was coupled to the wheel train (in order first to unlock the wheel and secondly to receive a brief impulse), the balance was completely independent of the wheel train and thus retained the freedom of isochronism linked to the very properties of the hairspring. This was the second main principle embodied in modern chronometers. Finally, there remained the compensation for temperature changes, which had previously been made by adjusting the effective length of the balance spring. Instead of this, Le Roy applied correction to the balance itself, as was the practice with pendulum wall clocks. The balance was fitted

Another view of the McGregor chronometer showing the spring barrel, fusee and chain, a system that ensures that the movement is under constant tension throughout the run of the main spring.

with two capillary tubes filled at the bottom with mercury (to give a large variation in weight) and at the top with alcohol (for rapid expansion); as the temperature varied, the change in their moment of inertia was exactly equal and opposite to the variation in that of the balance. Compensation of the balance, which was later achieved by the use of a bimetallic balance, constituted the third main principle of modern marine clock-making. Le Roy's clock was examined with great interest by the Academy of Science and tested on *l'Aurore*, a small vessel built specially for a scientific voyage in the North Sea and equipped at the expense of the Marquis de Courtanvaux, capitaine-colonel of the Swiss Guard (the King's personal bodyguard), amateur astronomer and member of the French Academy of Science. Two identical clocks by Le Roy were tested, but the voyage was too short and punctuated by too many spells in port for the quality of the clocks to be fully assessed, so that a second trial was carried out in 1768 aboard *l'Enjouée* during a quadrangular voyage in the Atlantic lasting five months. At the end of the voyage the results obtained were comparable with those achieved by Harrison with his No. 4 clock.

Le Roy was no longer alone in having his clocks tested, however. Berthoud, whose work we shall look at later, had proved the quality of his machines Nos. 6 and 8 upon the return of *l'Isis* from her trial voyage. Borda expressed a favourable opinion after reading the notes made by Fleurieu, who had accompanied the clocks, and it was decided to carry out comparative tests aboard *la Flore* to distinguish between the two clockmakers on their merits. Berthoud's No. 8 performed better than Le

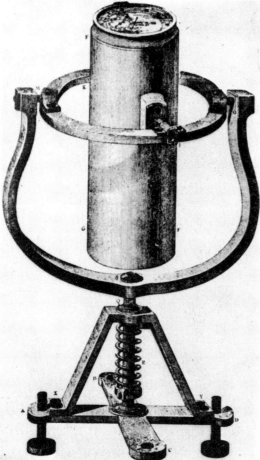

200. Weight-driven clock by F. Berthoud, showing the long case that was characteristic of this instrument and the gimbal mounting.

201. Marine chronometer, No. 68, by John Arnold and Sons, London. The octagonal walnut case is characteristic of the clocks produced by this clockmaker. Key winding through the base. Spring detent escapement. Cylindrical gold hairspring.

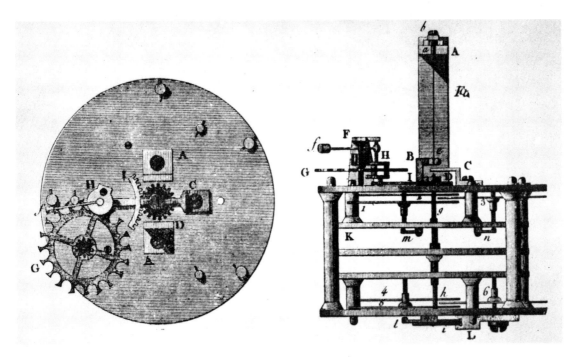

Roy's watches but it was Le Roy who received the prize as Berthoud, the official clockmaker to the Navy, could not compete, having been regularly commissioned to supply clocks of high quality.

Le Roy's work cannot be measured by the number of instruments he produced. Its value lies above all in the example and instruction it gave. Pierre Le Roy may be credited quite impartially with the invention of the modern chronometer – a term he coined, incidentally – in view of the three main principles mentioned above, which he was the first to combine happily in a single timekeeping machine.

Berthoud was cast in an entirely different mould. A skilful craftsman, clever at drawing attention to himself and accomplishing what others had established in principle but had not been able to translate into practice, he was certainly the most prolific clockmaker of his age. He also wrote important works which he considered worth publishing, partly as a means of better asserting the superiority of his achievements and ideas over those of his rival Pierre Le Roy. We have to wait until watch No. 52 to find Berthoud's instrument that is closest to the modern marine chronometer. There was great variety in the assembly of the various parts along the way: springs, hairsprings, weights, escapements, compensators, wheel trains . . . Everything was tried various ways, and it cannot be said that Berthoud concentrated on one particular aspect, as Harrison had been able to do, for example, with the remontoir or the escapement or Le Roy with his original ideas for the compensation or the detached escapement.

After the death of Harrison the work of the great clockmaker was continued in England by John Arnold (1736–1799) and Thomas Earnshaw (1749–1829), who solved the remaining problem of the escapement and in certain details reverted to designs that were simpler and more practicable for mass production, which was possible only with well-tried techniques. The same was being done in France by Abraham-Louis Breguet (1747–1823) and Louis Berthoud (1759–1813), the nephew of Ferdinand, as it was now essential to produce good longitude clocks for the Navy.

In 1832 the French Naval Ordnance listed 143 chronometers, by Berthoud, Breguet and Motel exclusively. The merchant navy still possessed none, and would not until about 1880.

202. Engravings reproduced from Traité des horloges marines *by Ferdinand Berthoud.* Right: *side view of the upper part of the movement.* Left: *view of the cylinder escapement used in marine clocks Nos. 6 and 8. AA' (here cut away) is the suspension of the regulator balance, the staff of which carries the pinion D. This receives the impulse from the escape wheel G via the cylinder H, which is fitted with ruby faces.*

203. Marine clock No. 3 by Berthoud, 1775. This clock was used by Borda in 1776.

The 1850s and 1860s saw the period of industrialisation, with the English clockmakers Frodsham, Dent, Ferguson, Cole and Denison, the Frenchmen Motel, Winnerl, Dumas, Vissière and Le Roy and the Swiss Dubois, Richard, Nardin and Jurgensen.

Does this mean that the French Navy indiscriminately bought chronometers made by the well-known firms as one would nowadays buy a quartz chronometer, with one's eyes closed, by relying on the good name of the maker and letting the instrument prove its worth in use?

In France there were initially clockmakers 'by appointment' to the Navy, such as Ferdinand and Louis Berthoud and later Breguet, who repaired

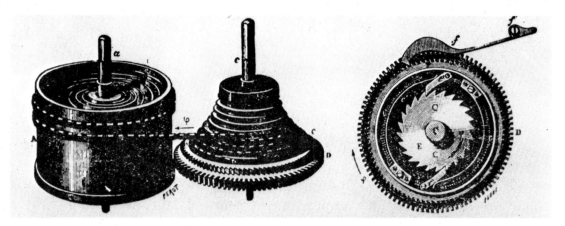

204. *Spring drum, chain, fusee, main spring and the device for maintaining the tension of the mechanism while it is being rewound. The conical shape of the fusee ensures that the leverage remains constant throughout the run of the spring.*

205. *Chronometer No. 94 by Louis Berthoud. It has three dials to show the hours, minutes and seconds.*

*206. Marine clock No. 36 by the
clockmaker Motel.*

longitude clocks and held them in store in the days before the establishment of the Naval Ordnance. As their output could not match demand, the title of supplier to the Navy was extended to include a number of other clockmakers, including Motel, the nephew of Louis Berthoud.

From 1833 onwards clocks were bought on the basis of competitive examination. The rules were difficult to draw up, but they were finally notified to the clockmakers. A price of Fr. 2,474 would be paid for the clocks chosen. In the first year forty-six clocks were selected; the rules were then modified on the basis of the trials carried out up to then on the clocks, not all of which could be taken to sea to be tried *in situ*. Attractive bonuses of up to Fr. 2,500 were offered for the best chronometers.

In 1858 the rules took on the form that would endure practically unchanged until the 1914–1918 war. In 1858 the Navy owned 57 Berthouds, 132 Motels, 71 Breguets, 56 Winnerls, 13 Roberts, 4 Daumas, 1 Lecoq, 11 Gannerys, 7 Vissières, 4 Rodanets, 2 Jacobs and eight English chronometers purchased for testing. The good watches with a second hand, which were called deck watches and were kept in a wooden case, were not long in coming.

The testing of chronometers at the time of purchase gradually declined in severity as radio time signals developed. From these the rate of the chronometers could be checked and the actual time recorded, and navigation did not suffer one little bit. At the same time it was easy to judge

Marine chronometer inverted to show the position for daily rewinding by means of the special ratchet key.

the variation of a particular timekeeper. The bad models or makers were quickly identified and eliminated from further purchases. Hence for the few large firms that continued to supply the Navy this was virtually a return to the system of privileges.

About a decade ago the large firms producing mechanical clocks ceased to make marine chronometers. Some shipping companies of the old school have kept their existing chronometers and reinstall them in new ships. Most large vessels leaving the shipyards today are equipped with quartz chronometers, but the extreme accuracy of these instruments is superfluous in our day and age, when good portable clocks can be adjusted quickly from a time signal, which can be obtained just as quickly on any radio receiver in any part of the world.

5 · Hydrography, Geodesy and Terrestrial Astronomy

207. Graphometer by Doizy.

Angle Measurements

208. *Graphometer by Baradelle, Paris.*

Maritime expeditions of discovery were very numerous in the second half of the 18th century and always carried a considerable amount of scientific equipment. The list of instruments that La Pérouse took with him has been preserved and is quoted by Daumas:

'Astronomical instruments, quadrants, transit instruments, telescopes, clocks, geodetic and topographical instruments, Borda reflecting circles, English sextants, theodolites, graphometers, sets of drawing instruments and various surveying and measuring implements. The expedition also took along the so-called 'Peruvian toise' which had been used by La Condamine and his colleagues. In addition there was a double-cylinder air pump, a plate electrical machine, both with all their accessories, barometers, hygrometers, thermometers, two Dellebare microscopes, a hydrostatic balance, eudiometers, a burning mirror, magnifying glasses, hydrometers, and finally a complete chemical laboratory with a furnace, retorts and chemicals . . .'.

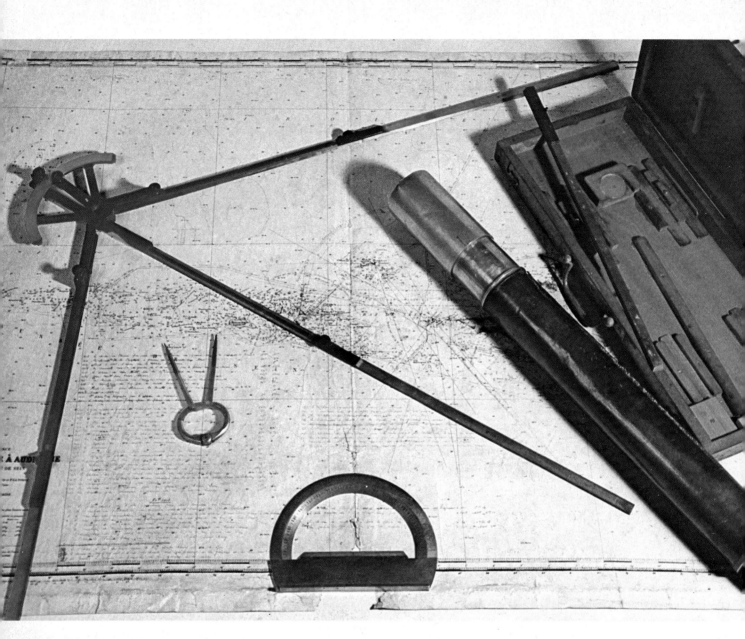

Station pointer positioned for plotting the bearings of the three landmarks Le Bouc, the Sein lighthouse and Ar Men. The value of this instrument lies in the fact that it can be used for plotting angular bearings taken with the hydrographic circle, which are thus free of errors of deviation and variation.

The station pointer is by A. Hurlimann, marked 'Marine A.G. 113'. The single draw ship's glass is signed 'W. F. Stanley, London, Day or Night'.

The protractor, bearing the number 94, is marked 'Hydrographic Department of the Soviet Navy'.

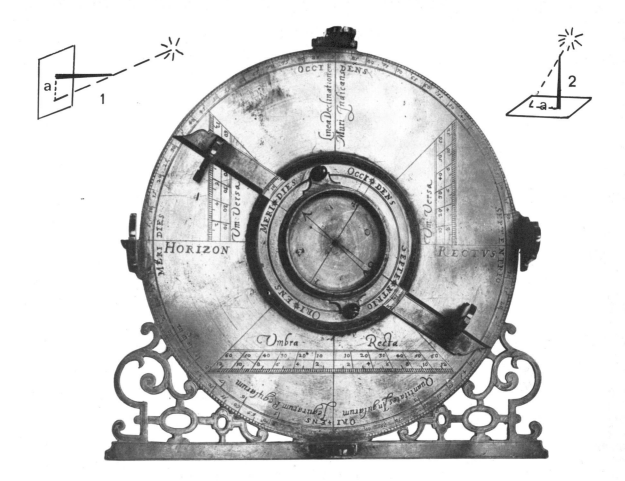

209. *16th-century circumferentor. The inscriptions* Umbra recta *and* Umbra versa *require some explanation. The Arabs represented tangents and cotangents as the projection of a unit gnomon. In the left-hand figure (1) the shadow gives the tangent a, or* umbra versa; *in figure 2 the shadow a represents the cotangent, or* umbra recta. *The length of the shadow, which is a multiple of that of the unit gnomon, is thus a trigonometric value. Around 1580–1600, however, the old name* umbra *fell into disuse and from then onwards only the terms tangent and cotangent were used.*

210. *Italian circumferentor.*

The longitude clocks, which had recently been acquired by the Navy, were the key instruments on these expeditions dispatched to check the geographic co-ordinates on the charts of the Naval Ordnance. In the case of France alone, mention must be made of the important hydrographic expeditions of Borda in 1776 along the coast of Africa and among the Canary Islands, of Rosily, Beautemps-Beaupré (1816–1826), Daussy, Roussin and Givry, to name but a few. Besides taking with them the tools of the new methods of navigation (clocks and chronometers), they also measured lunar distances with the reflecting circle and naturally cross-checked the precise measurements of longitude on land in the observatories that were established.

New instruments had appeared for plotting charts, such as the station pointer or instruments that were a cross between this and the parallel ruler.

Accurate Plotting

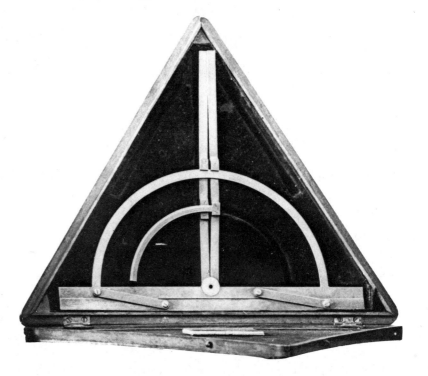

211. *A beautiful cased plotting instrument, without any indication of origin or date, consisting of parallel rulers and a movable arm protractor for hydrographic chart work.*

194

212. *Protractor with a movable arm by*
Troughton and Simms, London.

213. *Movable arm protractor, marked*
'Dépôt de la Marine'.

214. *Recipiangle or alidade protractor*
by Dulac, 1607.

Magnetic Inclination

Magnetic inclination was unknown until about the middle of the 16th century and when it was discovered it was considered to be of no value for navigation. At the beginning of the 19th century, however, interest revived as a result of the early attempts to plot isogonic lines and thereby to perfect navigation by the compass. Lines of equal inclination were plotted as well as those of equal variation, the direction and intensity of the field vector being of interest mainly to the proponents of the theory of a 'linear development' of terrestrial magnetism in time and place; as we know, this theory is a total

215. 19th-century dip circle by Gambey.

illusion, since the change is governed by no known laws.

Where a knowledge of inclination came into its own, however, was in the study of the rotating fields and coefficients associated with the magnetic influences on compasses aboard ship. For this the chart of the components of the Earth's magnetic field became indispensable.

Changes in the Earth's magnetism are still studied by direct measurement at sea, and it is not uncommon to discover anomalies.

216. *18th-century dipping needle by Magny.*

217. *Trade card of the firm of Ponthus et Therrode.*

218. *Serson's speculum, a form of artificial horizon. The mirror mounted in the case on a swivel joint has a square drive shaft. On the right is the spinning mechanism, comprising reduction gears and a belt that is pulled rapidly to set the mirror in motion.*

197

The Theodolite

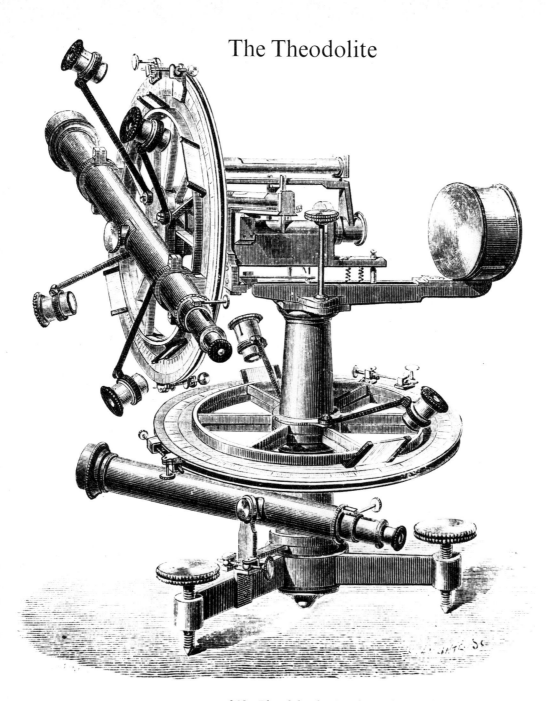

219. *Theodolite by Gambey. This geodetic instrument was designed for measuring zenith distances and angles in relation to the horizon. It has two graduated circles, one vertical with a telescope pivoting about a horizontal axis and the other horizontal with a vertical axis, also fitted with a telescope. Each circle consists of two rings, one fixed and the other movable, which can be locked together by means of a clamping screw. Normal practice is to take measurements by means of repeated and crossed observations. The bubble levels are used for adjusting the horizontals when setting up the instrument. The theodolite seems to have been a British invention, as the first instruments of any value made their appearance during the lifetime of the instrument maker Ramsden. Various forms exist, depending on the maker and the use to which surveyors put them, but the principle of the double measurement of the vertical and horizontal angles is common to them all.*

Measuring Circles

Not having fixed observatory instruments, the scientists on geographical expeditions took repeating circles with them, which were instruments for measuring angles in inclined planes. The main advantage of taking repeated angles with the circle lies in the almost infinitesimally close margin to which the angle can be measured by this method, in theory at least.

An angle measurement can be subject to two errors, namely in *sighting* and in *reading off*. The former is always very small (in the region of $1''$) whereas the latter is large, since angles cannot be read to less than one minute. Hence if a multiple of the required angle is measured instead of the angle itself and is read off only once, the result obtained will be out at most by only the error in reading off divided by n, the number of times the angle was measured.

220. Repeating circles.

In the Borda repeating circle the limb can be inclined in any direction required; the observer measures the angle in its plane instead of measuring its horizontal projection directly.

If this instrument is used, the reduction to the horizon must be calculated for each angle measured, which marks the essential difference between the circle and the theodolite.

221. Marine theodolite with pinhole sights and a telescope. The latter is missing, and all that can be seen at the top of the instrument are the two axle supports. It is hung in gimbals and there is a counterweight to ensure that the instrument remains vertical.

222. Repeating circle by Lenoir, 1805.

Artificial horizon (foreground, right) *in polished black marble with its bubble level, by E. Lorieux, Paris, No. 240. Cartographic Office of the Navy, France, end of the 19th century.*

   Mercury artificial horizon consisting of the trough with a stabilising channel, filler bottle and cover of non-prismatic panes of glass set at right angles. Signed 'Negretti & Zambra, Opticians, London'. End of the 19th century.

   The sextant is by G. Santi, Marseilles, end of the 19th century.

Marine Astronomy on Land

The astronomical sector was invented by Tycho Brahe (1546–1601) and subsequently improved; the example described in the *Encyclopédie* is by Picard. These instruments initially had sighting arms and were later fitted with telescopes; some of them have an enormous radius of more than two metres. Sometimes they are also called stand octants or sextants, depending on their angular capacity. The plane of the instrument can be pivoted, so that it can measure both vertical and horizontal angles; it can be used equally well for both surveying and astronomy.

The astronomical quadrant is often a fixed instrument of larger proportions than the sector but based on the same principle. It may be used as a transit instrument.

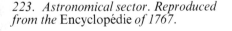

223. Astronomical sector. Reproduced from the Encyclopédie *of 1767.*

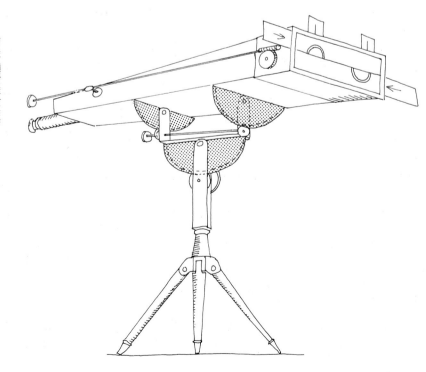

224. *Prismatic astrolabe by the Parisian instrument maker A. Jobin. This geodetic instrument for measuring equal altitudes applies the property of the equilateral triangle prism in place of the double mirror system used in reflecting instruments for measuring angles of one value, that of 60°.*

The part marked H is a trough of mercury, providing a perfect horizontal plane to reflect the image of the star towards the lower face of the prism A. The star is sighted direct at C. Collimation is performed by the telescope. Further details may be found in Description et usage de l'astrolabe à prisme *by Claude and Driencourt, published by Gauthier-Villars, 1910.*

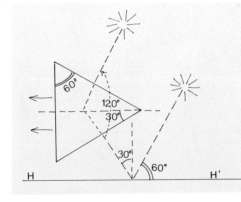

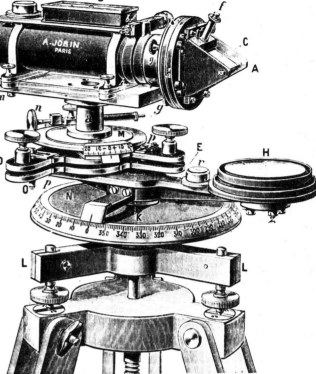

225. *When there is perfect collimation of the direct and reflected images through the prism the angle between the two beams of light is 120°, so that the star's altitude is 60°.*

◀ **226.** *The heliometer. In 1748 Bouguer suggested increasing the field of the heliometer to 3 or 4° so that the distances between the moon and stars in conjunction could be measured accurately. In 1767 Lt.-Cdr. Charnières produced a 'megameter' which he described in 1772 in his book on the subject. Made by Carochez, it cost 350 livres. The earliest model had divided object lenses by Dollond which moved in a straight line; in later versions they revolved through arcs of a circle with a common centre and equal radius. The object lenses had a diameter of 34 mm and a focal length of 208 cm. One lens was adjusted against the other by means of a tangent screw. The maximum arc that could be measured was 10–12° and the result was read to within a second of arc. Charnières proved the value of the instrument at sea during a voyage to Guadeloupe on the ship le Sensible in 1767. Messier tested the megameter on Courtanvaux's l'Aurore and Mersay used it during the voyage of Verdun de La Crène. The instrument could certainly be used at sea, but there were limitations imposed by the small number of stars close to the moon and by errors in reducing very small lunar distances. Hence the measurement of the angle was precise, but the final results of the calculations were no better than with measurements taken with the octant. Rochon had the idea of placing prisms with a known deviation in front of the object lenses in order to widen the field of measurement, but the heliometer remained an observatory instrument, not a navigational tool.*

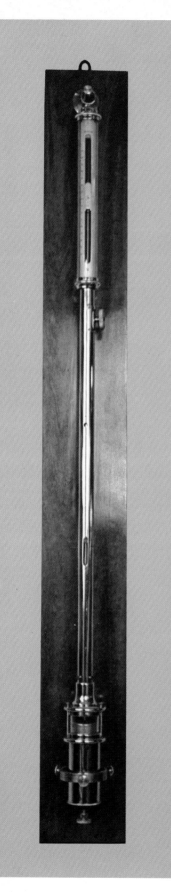

6 · Observing and Forecasting the Weather

Meteorological Instruments

The first scientific notions of meteorology emerged towards the middle of the 19th century. Matthew Fontaine Maury, the founder of the American Hydrographic Office, charted the winds and currents in his *Pilot Charts* and *Sailing Directions*. Nonetheless, local short-term forecasting was still no more than a pious hope. In any case, even if meteorological offices capable of making forecasts did exist, how were they to broadcast the information? In port storm signals are hoisted and in coastal waters seamen know from experience what weather to expect, but at sea it is quite another matter. Some areas, such as the North Atlantic, are frank about their fits of temper, and the harbingers of depressions speak to seamen, but off the coast of southern Brazil what cloud will warn of a white squall – invisible, by definition – or a blast of *pampero*? Or off the Gulf of Mexico with the finest weather in the world, how would you know that you were in the path of a hurricane? For centuries seamen spent the long hours on watch scrutinising the sky at dawn and dusk, observing changes in the colour of the sea, the direction of the waves and the angle of the wind vane at the masthead, judging the strength of the wind as much by sound as by the appearance of the white crests of the waves in order to build up an opinion of the weather. However clear an idea they may have had, it seems that from the time it came into existence they never challenged the indications of the barometer, which always showed itself prophetic in extreme cases.

The first reliable barometers were those with a tube and cistern that applied Torricelli's principle directly. The gimballed marine version first appeared at the beginning of the 19th century and had a relatively large cistern (Tonnelot). The Fortin type, which had a small cistern, proved to be less fragile and in fine weather gave very good readings if one could interpolate between the extreme positions of the mercury column as it rose and fell with the roll of the ship. In very heavy weather one had to be a magician to read the barometer, and so the circular corrugated metal box exhausted of air, called a Vidie capsule, was put to good use in so-called aneroid or holosteric barometers, which had either a dial or a recording drum; these were at least unaffected by the motion of the ship and although they tended to stick a little (a good excuse for tapping them with your finger as though to elicit a response) they were preferred aboard ship.

Invaluable indications could therefore be drawn from the direction and rate of change in pressure by reference to the general rules given in the *Sailing Directions*. The direction and strength of the wind is another essential feature of the weather forecast. There can be no doubt that in the days of sail seamen could judge it precisely from experience, by the tension of the rigging and the singing of the wind in the mast, but hydrographic and meteorological vessels could not be satisfied with human judgement, which by definition is subjective and imprecise. The anemometer, or wind speed indicator, has taken many forms, but the two basic principles of

Fortin mercury barometer, regulation issue in the French Navy, about 1880.

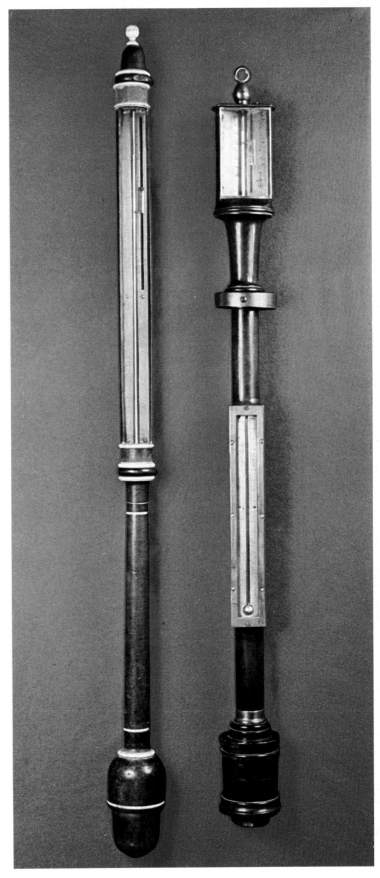

Two 18th-century marine barometers, one suspended from a ring and the other in gimbals.

TROISIEME LIVRE
DES VENTS, DE LEVRS NOMS
ET QVALITEZ, ET COMMENT ON
DOIT NAVIGVER PAR ICEVX.

227. Reproduced from the French translation of Arte de navegar *by Pedro de Medina.*

measurement are still the rotation of a wheel with blades or cups turning a revolution counter or alternatively the pressure of the wind on a calibrated surface. The latter type is represented just as well by a device consisting of a cup whose angle from the vertical is proportional to the strength of the wind as by instruments such as the Droinet velocimeter based on a drop in pressure.

In the days of sail seamen always distrusted the impression given by the apparent wind, which was deflected onto the poop deck by the sails; the ideal measurement seemed to be that taken at the masthead. Once electrical batteries had been invented a number of ingenious transmission systems were developed to relay information about the wind blowing at the truck of the mast.

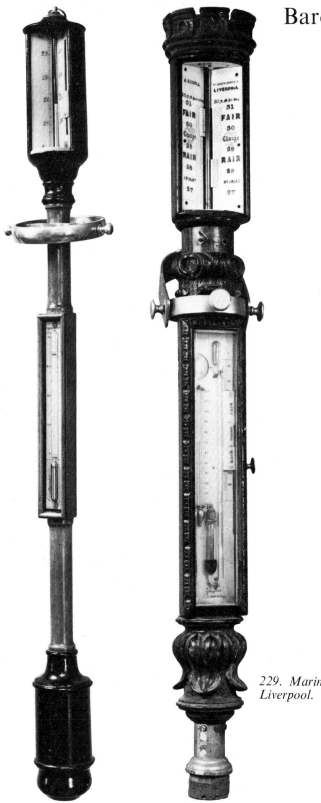

229. *Marine barometer by J. Sewill, Liverpool.*

230. *Barometer by Dollond, London.*

228. *English marine barometer, gimbal mounted, graduated in inches.*

Large barograph with eight vacuum boxes, very
beautifully made by Wilson and Harden, London.
Anemometer, 11 cm in diameter, by Winter of
Newcastle to Biram's Patent 148, end of the 19th
century. Rose showing the equivalences of points of
sailing and true headings according to the direction
of the wind, French, end of the 18th century.

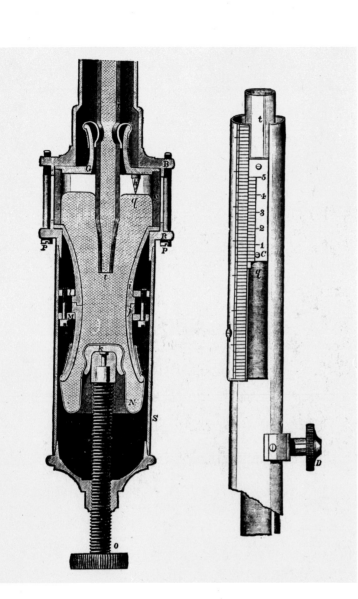

231. Cross-section of the Fortin barometer showing the cistern terminating in a chamois leather sac, which is pushed upwards by the screw O so that at q the mercury just touches the pointer h. Right: *the vernier for fine measurements to one-hundredth of an inch. At C the vernier just touches the top of the meniscus of the mercury column.*

232. Travelling barometer.

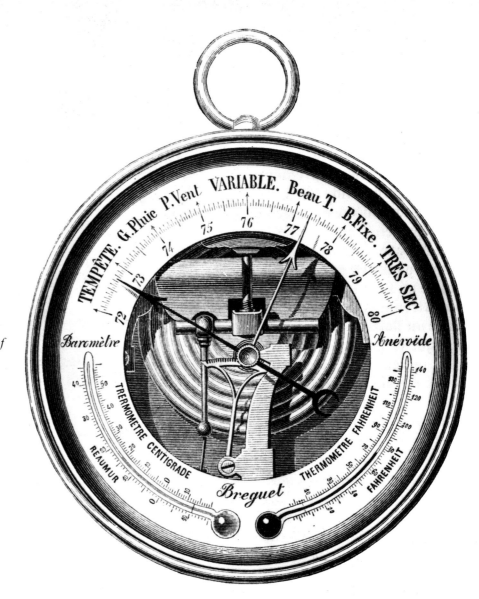

233. *Aneroid barometer by Breguet.*
The deformation of the vacuum box is
amplified to move the needle by means of
a toothed arc.

234. *Invoice from the firm of Jecker*
made out to 'Monsieur Robert Surcouf'
in July 1819.

The Speed and Direction of the Wind

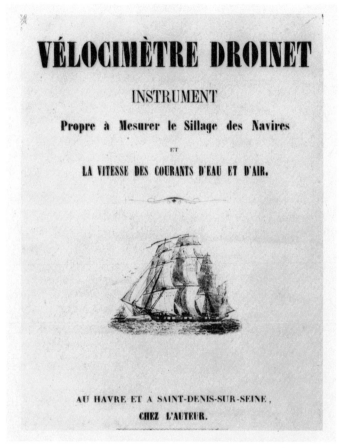

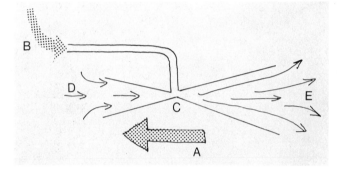

236. *The principle of the Droinet velocimeter: D and E intake and outlet of the stream of water; C Venturi tube; B suction and A direction of travel of the vessel.*

235. *The Droinet velocimeter. The following is an extract from the maker's comments on the trials of this instrument for measuring speed conducted aboard the yacht* Black Eagle *of the British Admiralty in August 1854 and on the French despatch boat* Galilée *in April 1855: 'Now that our instrument has successfully passed all the tests to which it could rightly be subjected and that we can produce authentic certificates and irrefutable testimony in support of each of the tests, we hasten to give it due publicity and to draw the attention of navigators to a new speedometer that gives continuous and mathematically accurate readings at all times and will never let them down.' The editor of the* Ami des sciences *wrote with reference to the velocimeter: 'This instrument is based on the principle of the constriction of the jet stream; in fact, it is simply an ingenious application of the double-cone Venturi tube. The tube is between 30 and 36 cm long and is fixed to the ship whose speed it is to measure. It consists of two truncated cones of different heights joined at their apices. At the junction of the two cones a small hole has been drilled and a narrow tube attached; as soon as the ship moves, suction is produced in the tube, increasing in proportion to the speed. The inventor had the idea of applying this suction to a pressure gauge; this could be a column of mercury with a graduated scale, a device based on the Vidie vacuum chamber or the Bourdon vacuum indicator.'*

The instruction booklet for the Velocimètre *contains other information about its use as an anemometer, in which guise it seems to have been fitted successfully to several ships of the French Navy.*

237. *Elementary cup anemometer, consisting of a direction vane and a scale showing the strength of the wind in terms of the angle of the arm.*

238. *Paddle wheel anemometer for mounting at the masthead, about 1880. The frame is designed to carry a wind vane. Note the bronze rollers on the upper bearing for frictionless movement. The speed is not measured continuously; a spring holds the gear wheels out of mesh with the endless screw driven by the paddles. The mechanism is brought into gear by hauling on a cable. The larger wheel is fitted with a peg that closes an electrical circuit connected to a bell. A table gives the speed of the wind in relation to the interval of time between rings.*

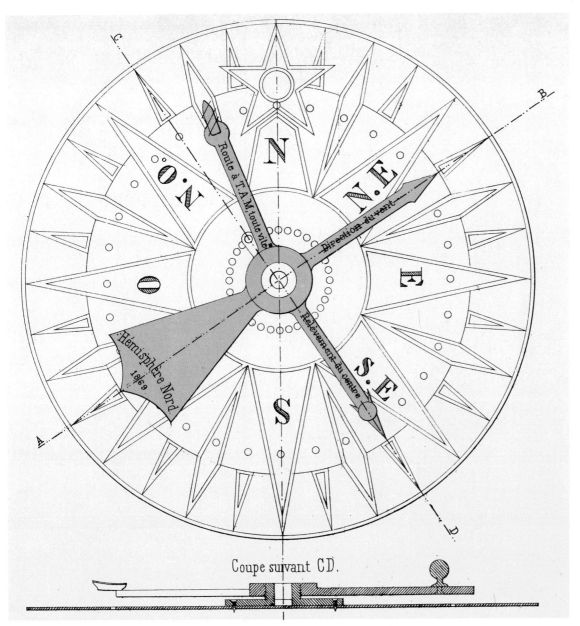

239. *The hurricane dial of Cdr. F.-R. Roux, about 1870. His book entitled* le
Guide des ouragans *contains the following passage about the instrument: 'As
storms are fortunately fairly rare, I had the idea of fitting two simple needles to the
hurricane dial, in appropriate positions, and thus converting it for use as a course
and bearing corrector. I have entrusted the execution of the instruments that I
have just described to the skilful Marseilles optician Monsieur Santi. The first
examples shown to me are remarkable in their precision and finish; they leave
nothing to be desired. As I have inspected the moulds from which they came and
checked all the lettering and instructions, the navigator may have absolute
confidence in the products bearing the mark of this reputable manufacturer. This
recommendation is made solely in view of counterfeits. As for myself, I expect no
recompense from my work other than the satisfaction of having rendered a service
to the great family of mariners, to which I am honoured to belong.'*

*Further details on this multi-purpose device, which was typical of the
instruments produced during that era, can be found in the* Revue maritime et
coloniale *of August 1870.*

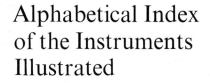

Alphabetical Index of the Instruments Illustrated

(As a rule the numbers relate to the illustrations; those preceded by the letter p *relate to the pages on which colour prints appear.)*

Alidade *see* Compass, bearing
Anemometer, p208, 235–238
Armillary sphere, p4, 84, 151
Artificial horizon, 132–135, 138, 218, p201
Astrolabe, 93, 94, p152
Astrolabe, prismatic, 224, 225

Back-staff, 99, 100, 102–104, p116
Barograph, p208
Barometer, p204, p205, 228–233
Binnacle, p28, p29, 24, 25, p32, 26, 27, 29, 30, 32, 36

Chart, 57
Chronometer, p177, p180, p181, 201, p185, 205, p188, p189
Circumferentor, 209, 210
Clock,
  cycloidal pendulum, 192
  marine, 193, 194, 198–200, 202, 203, 206
Compass,
  azimuth *see* Compass, bearing
  bearing, 1, 17–21, 167
  boat's, 9, 22, 28
  Chinese, p9
  dory, p88
  dry-card, 3, 8, 10, 11, 18, 19, 25, p32
  liquid, 28, p41, p88
  overhead, 10
  registering, p36
  ring magnet, 13
  steering, p28, p29, 26, 27, p64
  tell-tale *see* Compass, overhead
  variation, 20
Compass card, p13, p16, 11, 12, 14–16, p25, 242–244
Compass needle, 12, 14
Compendium, astronomical, 191
Cosmolabe, 85–87
Course corrector, 37, 38
Course recorder, 34
Crossbow, 106
Cross-staff, 96–98, p117

Depth sounder, 69, 72, 73 *see also* Sounding fly
Dials *see* Sundials
Dial, hurricane, 239
Dip circle, 215
Dipping needle, 216
Dividers, four-armed, 88
Drawing instruments, p44
Dromoscope, 35 *see also* Course corrector

Elongating lens, 139
Escapement, 195, 196

240. *This strange device for improving dead-reckoning calculations, pompously termed a 'copper leeway indicator with pinnules', was lashed to the taffrail by its two arms; the pointers on the alidade could then be used to estimate the leeway by taking a bearing of the wake. On sailing ships this piece of information played a very important part in calculating the course.*

Flinders bar, p29
Fog horizon, 138
Forestaff *see* Cross-staff
Fusee, 204

Globe,
    celestial, p81
    star, p88, 140
    terrestrial, p129
Graphical operator, 66
Graphometer, 207, 208

Heliometer, 226
Hemisphere, nautical, 90
Hydrometer, Foxon's, 45

Jacob's staff *see* Cross-staff

Leeway indicator, 240
Lodestone, 4–7
Log,
    electrical, 54, 55
    rotating, p41, 45–52
    taffrail, p41, 48, 52
    towing *see* Log, rotating
Log-glass *see* Sand-glass
Log ship, 39, 40

Micrometer, 82, 83

Nocturnal, p164, p165, 183–190

Observation chair, 86
Octant, 107–112, p97, 113–115, p100,
    118–121, p104, 125, 134
Orrery *see* Planetarium

Planetarium, p81
Planisphere, 150
Position-finding machine, 128
Protractor, p41, p192, 211–213

Quadrant,
    Davis *see* Back-staff
    Elton's, 132
    Gunter, p84, p85, 95
    Hadley *see* Octant
    mariner's, 63
    nautical, 106
    shipman's *see* Square, nautical
    sinical *see* Quadrant, mariner's
Quintant, 137

Recipiangle, 214
Reflecting circle, p120, 144, 145, 147,
    148, 168
Repeating circle, 220, 222
Rhumb lines, p12, 16, 241
Rose of equivalences, p208
Rule, rolling, p44, 67, 68
Rulers, parallel, 67, 211
Running glass *see* Sand-glass

Sand-glass, p133, p136, 152–154
Sector, p44, 59–61

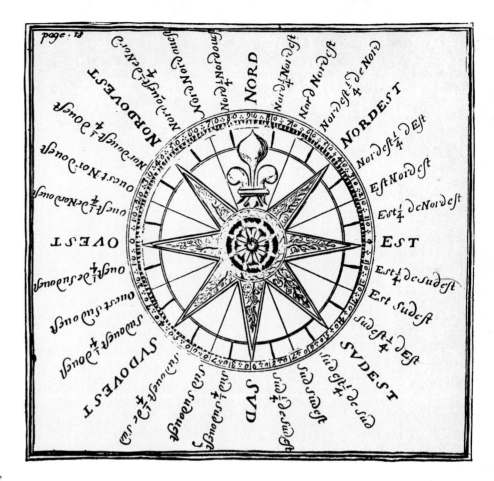

241. *Division of the compass rose into the rhumbs of the wind; from* la Pratique du pilotage *by Father Pezenas, 18th century.*

Sector, astronomical, 223
Serson's speculum, 132, 218
Sextant, p101, 123, 126, 127, 129–131,
    p113, 138, 139, p201
    artificial horizon, 133
    bubble, 138
    double, 136
    gyroscopic, 135
    pocket, 141
Sounding fly, 70–73
Sounding machine, 76, 77
Speedometer, 42–44, 56, 235, 236
Square, nautical, 62
Station pointer, 66, p192
Sundial,
    analemmatic, 156
    azimuth, 155
    Butterfield, 160
    cylinder *see* Sundial, pillar
    diptych, 157
    equinoctial, p132, 158, 164, 169, 170
    equinoctial ring, 177–182
    horizontal plate, 159
    mean time, 171

mechanical equinoctial, 164, 170
    pillar, 161
    polar, 163
    ring, 172–176
    shepherd *see* Sundial, pillar
    universal, p132
    universal ring *see* Sundial,
    equinoctial ring
    vertical, 162

Taximeter, 31
Telescope, p44, 78–81, p192
Theodolite, 219
Theodolite, marine, 221
Tides calculator, p152
Timekeeper *see* Chronometer, Clock,
    Watch
Timer, log, 41
Traverse board, p44, p48, p61, 63

Velocimeter, 235, 236
Vernier, 120, 121

Watch, longitude, 197

Bibliography

Abrizzi, *Introduzzione all'arte nautica.*
Anderson R. G. W., *The Mariner's Astrolabe,* Edinburgh, 1972
Anthiaume A. et Sottas J., *l'Astrolabe quadrant au Musée des Antiquités de Rouen,* Paris, 1910.
Apian, *Cosmographia.*

Becborrow, *The Longitude not Found,* 1678.
Bellin, *Petit Atlas maritime,* Paris, 1764.
Bernouilli J., *Lettres astronomiques.*
Berthoud F., *Traité des horloges marines,* Paris, 1773; *Histoire de la mesure du temps par les horloges,* Paris, 1802; *Supplément au traité des montres à longitude,* Paris, 1807.
Berthoud L., *Entretiens sur l'horlogerie,* Paris, 1812.
Besson J., *Théâtre des instruments mathématiques et mécaniques.*

Bezout, *Cours de navigation,* Paris, 1814.
Bion N., *Traité de la construction et des principaux usages des instruments de mathématique,* 1725.
Bird J., *The Method of Dividing Astronomical Instruments,* London, 1768.
Blondel de Saint-Aubin, *l'Art de naviguer par le quartier de réduction,* 1671.
Bloud C., *Usage de l'horloge ou quadran azimutal, ensemble de l'équinoctial,* Dieppe, 1668.
Bond, *The Longitude Found,* 1676; *Norwood's Epitome,* 1645.
Borda, *Description du cercle de réflexion,* Paris, 1816.
Bory, *Description du nouveau quartier anglais,* Paris, 1751.
Bouguer, *Nouveau Traité de navigation, Traité complet de navigation,* Paris, 1781.
Bourne W., *A Regiment for the Sea,* London, 1577.
Brewington M. V., *The Peabody Museum Collection of Navigating Instruments,* Salem, 1963.

Caillet, *Traité de navigation,* Paris, 1868.
Cassini, *Voyage fait en 1768 pour éprouver les montres de Le Roy,* Paris, 1770.

Chabert, *Voyage en 1750 et 1751 dans l'Amérique septentrionale,* Paris, 1753.
Charnières, *Traité et pratique des longitudes à la mer,* Paris, 1772.
Claude A. et Driencourt L., *Description et usage de l'astrolabe à prisme,* Paris, 1910.
Coignet M., *Instruction nouvelle de l'art de naviguer,* Antwerp, 1581.
Collet, *Traité de la régulation et de la compensation des compas,* Paris, 1882.
Cotter Ch. H., *A History of Nautical Astronomy,* London, 1968.
Courtanvaux, *Journal du voyage de 'l'Aurore',* Paris, 1768.

Danfries Ph., *Déclaration du graphomètre,* Paris, 1597.
D'Après de Mannevilette, *le Nouveau Quartier anglais,* Paris, 1739.
Dassié F., *le Pilote expert,* 1683.
Daumas M., *Les instruments scientifiques au XVIIe et XVIIIe siècles,* Paris, 1953.
Davis J., *The Seaman's Secrets,* 1595.
De Gaulle, *Nouveau compas azimutal à réflexion,* Le Havre, 1779.
Delambre, *Astronomie théorique et pratique,* Paris, 1814.
Destombes M., articles sur l'hydrographie et l'astrolabe, in *Neptunia. Catalogue des cartes nautiques sur vélin,* Paris, B.N., 1963.
Dujardin-Troadec L., *les Cartographes bretons du Conquet, 1543–1650.*

Engbert S. E., *Descriptive Catalogue of Telescopes.*

Fleurieu, *Voyage fait en 1768 et 1769 pour éprouver les montres de F. Berthoud,* Paris, 1773.
Fournier P., *Hydrographie,* Paris, 1643.

Gaigneur, *le Pilote instruit,* Nantes, 1781.
Garcia Franco S., *Instrumentos nauticos en el Museo Naval,* Madrid, 1959.
Guépratte, *Vade-mecum du marin,* Brest, n.d.
Guillaume le Nautonnier, *Mécométrie de l'aymant,* 1603.
Gunter, *The Description and Use of the Sector.*

242, 243. Compass cards.

Guye S. et Michel H., *Mesure du tempts et de l'espace*, Paris, 1970.
Guyou, *Manuel des instruments nautiques*, Paris, 1870.

Lalande J., *Abrégé de navigation*, Paris, 1793.
Le Calvé A., *Cours d'astronomie nautique*, Paris, 1946.
Le Cordier, *Instruction des pilotes*, 1683.
Ledieu, *Nouvelles Méthodes de navigation*, Paris, 1877.
Lemonnier, *Lois du magnétisme*, Paris, 1776. *Instructions astronomiques. Description et usage des principaux instruments d'astronomie.*
Le Roy, *Précis des recherches faites en France depuis 1730 pour déterminer la longitude à la mer par la mesure artificielle du temps*, Amsterdam, 1773.
Lévêque, *le Guide du navigateur*, 1779.

Magellan, *Description des octants et sextants anglais*, Paris, 1775.
Marguet F., *Histoire générale de la navigation. Du XVe au XXe siècle*, Paris,1931; *Cours de navigation et de compas de l'Ecole navale*, Paris, 1938; *Histoire de la longitude à la mer*, Paris, 1917.
Medina P. de, *Arte de navegar*, Valladolid, 1545.
Mendoza, *Memoria sobre algunos métodos de calcular la longitud*, Madrid, 1795.
Metius A., *Astronomical Institution*, 1605.
Michel H., *les Instruments des sciences*, Paris, 1966.

National Maritime Museum Greenwich, *Navigation and Astronomy Instruments.*
Norwood, *The Seaman's Practice*, 1637.

Pagel, *la Latitude par les hauteurs hors du méridien.*
Pezenas, *la Pratique du pilotage, Astronomie des marins*, 1765; *Mémoires de mathématiques*, 1755.
Polak J., *Bibliographie maritime française*, Paris, 1976.

Ramsden J., *Description d'une machine pour diviser les instruments de mathématique*, Paris, 1790.
Rochon A. M., *Recueil de mémoires sur la mécanique et la physique*, Paris, 1783.

Rooseboom M., *Bijdrage tot de geschiedenis der instrument makerkunst in de noordelijke nederlanden tot omstreeks, 1840.*

Saunier, *Traité d'horlogerie*, Paris, 1872.
Saverien, *l'Art de mesurer le sillage du vaisseau*, Paris, 1750.
Sonnet H., *Dictionnaire des mathématiques appliquées*, Paris, 1867.
Stevin, *Hypomnemata mathematica*, 1608.

Turner E., *Van Marum's Scientific instruments in Teyler's Museum.*

Valois Y., *la Science et la pratique du pilotage*, 1735.

Waters David W., *The Art of Navigation in England in Elizabethan and Early Stuart Times*, London, 1958.
Werner J., *Commentaires sur la geographie de Ptolémée*, 1514.
Whiston W., *The Longitude & Latitude Found by the Inclinatory or Dipping Needle*, London, 1721.
Wright R., *Certain Errors in Navigation Detected and Corrected*, London, 1599.
Wynter H. and Turner A., *Scientific Instruments*, London, 1975.

244. Compass card.

Acknowledgements

J.-M. Arthaud, Cdt L.-M. Bayle, A. Brieux, J.-P. Busson, J.-H. Chambon (†), M. Cordelier, H. Cras, H. de Finfe, A. de Vos, S. Galanis, Mr Hazelhoff, Kelvin-Hughes, N. Kramer, Mr Labar, D. Lailler, Dr J. Meyer, A. Morel, W. F. J. Mörzer Bruyns, A. Paviot, Mr Petitcollot, Plath Sextant Hamburg, H.-C. Randier, Mr Redouté, Service historique de la Marine, Vincennes, Mr Soulard, Studio Duffort, Studio Gorne, G. Suc, J. Van Beylen, Wempe Chronometerwerke.

Sources of the Photographs

List of Museums

Great Britain
British Museum, London.
Museum of the History of the Sciences, Oxford.
National Maritime Museum, Greenwich.
Royal Observatory, Greenwich.
Royal Scottish Museum, Edinburgh.
Science Museum, London.
Whipple Museum, Cambridge.

Belgium
Nationaal Scheepvaartmuseum, Antwerp.

Denmark
Sofarts Museet, Copenhagen.

France
Conservatoire National des Arts et Metiers, Paris.
Musée de la Marine, Paris.
Musée de l'Observatoire, Paris.
Musée international du long-cours cap-hornier, Saint-Malo/Saint-Servan.
Service Hydrographique de la Marine, Brest.

Germany
Altonaer Museum, Hamburg.
Deutsches Museum, Munich.
Schiffahrts Museum, Brake/Unterweser.

Holland
Leyden Museum.
Maritime Museum, Rotterdam.
Rijksmuseum, Amsterdam.
Scheepvaart Museum, Amsterdam.
Teylers Museum, Haarlem.
University Museum, Utrecht.

Italy
History and Science Museum, Florence.
Museo Storico Navale, Venice.
Science Museum, Milan.

Portugal
Museu de Marinha, Lisbon.

Spain
Museo Marítimo, Barcelona.
Museo Naval, Madrid.

Sweden
Sjöfarts Museet, Göteborg.
Statens Sjöhistoriska, Stockholm.

Switzerland
Musée International d'horlogerie, La Chaux-de-Fonds.

United States
Mariners Museum, Newport News.
Maritime Museum, San Francisco.
Museum of Sciences, Boston.
Smithsonian Institution, Washington, D.C.
U.S. Naval Academy Museum, Annapolis.

U.S.S.R
Vojenno-Marskoi Moezjei, Leningrad.